MASTERY OF ABUNDANT LIVING

The Key to Mastering the Law of Attraction

Bruce Goldwell & Tammy Lynch

ISBN 978-1-894936-79-8
Copyright © 2007 Bruce Goldwell and Tammy Lynch
© 2007 Mastery Source, LLC, All Rights Reserved
Saga Books
Sagabooks.net
Cover Art by RT

Endorsements:

"Wow, this new book by Bruce Goldwell and Tammy Lynch is right in sync with my own '*Think Rich!*' message! Indeed it treats wonderfully of that HoloMagic "c2" factor! It brings to light so many aspects of the "Law *of Attraction*" that any one who is seriously (or only casually) interested in USING that Law to receive money and abundance in their lives *MUST* read it! It's so good I'm going to start recommending it as a companion to ' *The NEW Think And Grow Rich!"* **Ted Ciuba**, author of best-selling "*The NEW Think and Grow Rich*"

"A powerful read. This information will change many lives." **John P. Strelecky**, International Best Selling Author, *"The Why Café"*

"Abundance is a mind set and heart set. Abundance is ours for the asking...and doing. The Law of Fair Exchange teaches us that you will receive in proportion to your efforts. Tammy and Bruce have set this book up in such a way the you can have abundance by first, making a decision to be abundant, and then follow the step-by-step formula. Can you have abundance NOW? Maybe. Truthfully, it will take as long as it takes. Every idea, thought or creation has a gestation period. An idea cannot grow unless the seed is planted. Plant your seed for abundance then nurture it until you're there. It will be worth it." **Barry Spilchuk** - Founder "You're My Hero [TM]" Books and Co-author of "A Cup of Chicken Soup for the Soul"

"Bruce and Tammy have hit one out of the ball park with their new book '*Mastery of Abundant Living*'. This book will take readers into a whole new realm in dealing with the Law of Attraction . My first impression is - WOW!" **Linda Forsythe**, Publisher/Founder of *Mentors Magazine* & the *'Walking With the Wise'* book series

"The '*Mastery of Abundant Living'* is an incredible book that teaches the reader how to apply the Universal Law of Attraction to everyday life! It provides easy to follow principles as well as practical and inspirational information that will literally change your thinking, hence change your outcomes permanently." **Matthew J. Loop, DC**, author of *'Cracking the Cancer Code'*

CONTENTS

Part 1

1. I Live In An Abundant Universe
2. My Outer World Is Determined By My Inner World
3. My Thoughts Control My Destiny - I Only Nurture Thoughts That Are In Accord With Harmonic Abundance
4. I Release Any And All Barriers Both Conscious And Un-Conscious
5. When I Create Ideal Visions And Rehearse My Future, I Am Presented With Ideal Opportunities That Match My Intention
6. I Allow The Possibilities To Unfold Before Me And Am Inspired Down The Right Path

Part 2

7. How Do I Apply the Law of Attraction?
8. A Guide to Meditation
9. Creating Abundant Health
10. Manifesting Abundant Wealth
11. Attracting Abundant Love
12. Quantum Physics Basics
13. Vision Statements for Life
14. Personal Stories of Success
15. Conclusion

CHAPTER 1

"I Live In An Abundant Universe"

The Universe Has Everything It Needs To Prosper

All you have to do is go outside on a dark cloudless night and look up into the sky and you will see tens of thousand of stars and galaxies far off in the cosmos shining in all their wondrous glory. With the Hubble telescope, we can peer even deeper into our Universe and see the breathtaking images of stars, galaxies, constellations and other formations in space in limitless numbers.

The first principle we will explore, which is the beginning of our journey in attaining the *"Mastery of Abundant Living,"* is that we live in a Universe that is filled with abundance. Have you ever looked up at the sky at night and marveled in the number of stars shining down on you? It's possible that at one time in most of our lives; everyone has looked up and asked the question, "I wonder how many stars there are up there?" If we could pick a figure for the number of stars just in our corner of the Universe, it would be a number with so many zeros that it would be mind-boggling.

While the amount of real estate available in your town and even on this planet has its limits, the amount of real estate available in the Universe is *limitless*. The amount of matter and molecules that encompass the structure of our galaxy might have its limitations; however the Universe itself has *no limits*.

Our planet is just one speck of mud circling around a fiery sun that has almost a dozen planets circling about it. That sun, however, also circles around another group of worlds that circle around an even larger mass of space dust, particles and matter that make up more stars, planets, suns and space matter. The further we go out into space, the larger that mass of circulating planets, stars, suns and space matter becomes. Each time we move further out into space, the higher the number of entities in the circulating mass becomes until it grows to a number that is so large it is almost inconceivable.

When you only focus your attention on this world rather then the Universe as a whole, there is a tendency to think in finite terms. A child that lives in a neighborhood and never ventures beyond only sees what is in his or her immediate surroundings.

When a parent takes a child to the store, on a walk through the neighborhood, or to some other place outside the immediate area of the home, the child starts to become aware of the fact that there is more to the world then just Mom, Dad and the homes along the street. The further we venture out, the more we become aware of all the other things in this world.

We have the opportunity to discover through many means. We explore through books when we enter school, and television, movies and the Internet in a way that earlier generations never had the opportunity to do. There is so much to observe and learn about that it will take a lifetime just to see and understand a minute portion of it. We can observe things in the oceans, on land, under a microscope, through a telescope and so much more and it would take years just to get a glimpse of a small fraction of what can be seen. For those people that travel the world in hopes of visiting every country on the planet, it takes them a lifetime just to accomplish such a feat.

So how can we live in abundance if there is a limit to the matter that comprises our immediate world? The fact is that that matter constantly keeps changing form. The matter that is in the ground at one time may be the matter that makes up an apple, a peach, or some vegetable that will be eaten by a human, animal or insect, which will transform that matter again. Or it might just fall from the tree and again return to the ground only to resurface again in some other form as something useful. It is an endless cycle that has continued throughout time in this world and throughout the Universe for tens of thousands of years.

Nature itself always produces in abundance. Cut a tomato open and count the number of seeds that it has in it. Count the number of plants that could be produced from the seeds of that one tomato and then how many more tomatoes would be produced in just one year from those plants. There was a study that showed that if they took the seeds from one tomato and planted them, and then took the seeds from all the tomatoes from the first crop and repeated the process of growing crops from the seeds for three consecutive crops, that it would feed the world for one year from all the tomatoes that would be produced. That is abundance!

When we refer to the mastery of abundant living, we consider all aspects of what abundance entails. We don't just mean tons of food on the table and a storehouse of cash. Abundant living is living in a fullness of capacity in all areas of life: physically, emotionally, psychologically, intellectually and spiritually. This is called *"harmonic abundance."* If you are abundant in one area of life but lacking in another area, you are not living in *harmonic abundance.* The purpose of what is being shared with you is to improve your capacity to receive abundance in every aspect of your being.

Reprogramming your mind so that non-productive behavior is replaced by positive productive behaviors can do this. Becoming aware of the fact that we live not only in an abundant Universe but we live in an abundant world as well, you will begin to transform your thinking which will lead you into a realm where prosperity and abundance is the expectation and not the exception. As long as you continue to think that there is a shortage or a limitation to what is available, you will continue to be short changed when it comes to reaping from the harvest of those abundant resources.

We live in an abundant Universe and we live in an abundant world. The sooner you understand this principle, the sooner you can start to draw from its rich resources. There is always abundance. It is all around us. The fact that many people live in lack is not due to a shortage of resources but rather a shortage in their way of thinking. Somewhere along the way, we began to think that the Universe was lacking in what we all needed to survive and be happy. Somehow many in society believe that in order to have abundance, we have to compete for it. Why is this so?

The answer to this question has as many responses as there are beliefs in how we were created. Many of society's beliefs originated from science or religion. Because of this, references to both will be used throughout to help you understand why many of us today have the disempowering beliefs that have lead to a life of lacking, versus the life of abundance that everyone has a right to attain.

It is our objective to show you how to work within the Universal Laws, regardless of your religious belief, in order for you to begin living an abundant life.

When you consider that everything is in abundance in the Universe, and we individually are part of the Universe, why do you think that some live in abundance and others do not? It's simply because we have chosen it that way. That's correct. Our *free will* has allowed us to decide that this is the way it is.

Most people would agree that God, or the Universe if you prefer, creates through individuals. If you believe in the theory of evolution, then you certainly believe that we adapt based on growth and creation.

Regardless of your belief, creation occurs through individuals. Free will, as most would agree is our natural state of being, and ultimately our ability to think and decide for ourselves is part of the creative process. Free will is a key factor in most people's belief of how the Universe continues to grow and expand. Our different preferences make way for new creations.

Therefore, if everything is in abundance in the Universe, yet you're not living an abundant life, and creation occurs through the individuals, the fact that some are lacking and not living an abundant life is a *creation of the individual*.

When you think abundance, abundance is part of your life. When you think of lack, then there is lack in your life. You must choose if you are going to live in abundance or live in lack and that is a matter of *thought*.

To live in an abundant world, we must be abundant in what we already have. If we are employed and have a job that we work at either part-time or full-time, it behooves us to produce in an abundant way. If you are just doing enough to get by so you can receive a paycheck, then all that you will attract is enough to get by. This is <u>not</u> living abundantly!

When your work is abundant, you will find that a promotion or better job opportunity will present itself. The **Law of Abundance** guarantees that when you are abundant that more abundance will be presented to you. By living an abundant lifestyle, you will find that more and more abundance begins to come your way.

One of the very first scriptures given to man about abundance is in Genesis 9:7: "... be ye fruitful, and multiply; bring forth *abundantly* in the earth, and multiply therein."

To him who has will be given more but to him who hath not will be taken away. We live in a world where the rich keep getting richer and the poor keep getting poorer. This is not by some act of man, accident, or some government default that this occurs. This is based on the **Law of Abundance**. You attract more abundance when you are living the law and you repel abundance when you avoid being abundant yourself.

> Is there a lack of resources? NO.
> Is there a lack of money? NO.
> Is there a lack of opportunity? NO!

The answer to any question that has to do with lack will always and without fail be no! The only reason for lack in any individual's life is based on the individual's thoughts and expectations. When one thinks abundance and lives accordingly they will bask in abundance. When one thinks of lack and neediness, they will always be needy and lack in abundance.

MY THOUGHTS:

MY THOUGHTS:

CHAPTER 2

"My Outer World Is Determined By My Inner World"

Another key factor in the *Mastery of Abundant Living* is the understanding of your reality and how it comes to be. What comes into our lives as physical manifestations is always based on thoughts that we have nurtured over time. "Sew a thought, reap an act." For every thought there is a corresponding manifestation. "For every action, there's a reaction." Thought is the action, and the corresponding manifestation is the reaction. Thought is the cause, and your reality is the effect. When you learn to control your thoughts, you will be able to have things that manifest into your life that are in line with your true desires.

> *"Nothing splendid has ever been achieved except by those who dared believe that something inside of them was superior to circumstance."*   ~Bruce Barton

Answer this question. Who are you? Your answer will likely start with "I am…."

Who is the "I" in your statement? Is it your mind? Is it your body? Is it your personality?

Your mind is the computer or the mechanism that reasons, plans and responds to the "I."

Your body simply responds to the commands of the "I." I am going to walk here...or there. I'm going to go outside. Your body goes here or there, and it uses your subconscious mind to know how to walk, but it's the "I" that decides to walk. It's the "I" that is telling the body to walk, run, sit, or whatever. The "I" is the one making the decision as to what the body is going to do.

Could the "I" be your personality? Your personality is developed over time and is based on all life experiences, knowledge and basically everything and everyone you have experienced. Your personality is a result of your former thoughts. However, even your personality isn't the "I" that thinks.

The "I" in "I am" is the very nucleus of your existence. The "I" is the core of who you are. The "I" is what determines the direction you will head in life and the level of your accomplishments.

The "I" within you is something beyond the mind, body or personality. When you say "I want" or "I think," the "I" tells the mind what it wants or thinks. The "I" tells your body what to do. The "I" helps shape your personality based on preferences of the "I," but none of these things is the "I" within you. So then, who or what is the "I" that decides for you?

The "I" is your spirit, or your soul. It is the part of you that is united with everything and everyone in the Universe. It is the "I" that is part of the Infinite. The Infinite that has unlimited resources and everything in abundance.

Most religions and scientists commonly accept that there is a Higher Power or Eternal Energy that unites us. Scientifically, nothing is more certain that we are in the presence of an Infinite and Eternal Energy in which we are all connected. From a religious perspective, most consider God as being within us, and everywhere. The Bible says, "Know ye not that ye are the temple of the living God?" There are many times the Bible makes reference to God being within you. "*I AM* the Shepherd." "I and my Father are One." And so on…

Here in lies the "SECRET" of *The Mastery of Abundant Living*…the "I" within you is this Higher Power or Eternal Energy within you. It is All Powerful, has unlimited resources and has everything in abundance. This simple understanding is essential to most that have learned to *Master* the **Law of Attraction**.

For most, it's easy to believe that our Higher Power is willing and able to guide us to that in which we ask for, don't you agree?

So why is it then that sometimes we have things that appear in our lives and we think, "I didn't ask for that. I wanted something completely different."

The difficulty has been as simple as how we ask. Unfortunately, most of us have <u>not</u> been taught how to think correctly, or how to ask for what we desire. Most haven't been shown or taught how to use this *Unlimited Power* within us, and therefore, we don't receive what we want. We receive what we focus upon.

For example, many people who want to become healthier and decide that they want to lose weight constantly think and speak about food, and how much over weight they are. They want to be thinner, but they focus upon how heavy they are. They intend to diet really hard, and sacrifice. They compromise by eating what they don't like, and doing dreadful exercises. They know it will be difficult to become the weight they desire, and realistically, they don't ever expect to achieve it, but they'll give it their best shot.

Unfortunately, they expect exactly what they get and what they'll continue to get as long as they expect it. We have to change our thinking from wishing and hoping to intending and expecting.

Money and time are two things most believe they don't have enough of, wouldn't you agree? When you say you don't have the money for this or the time for that, you set yourself up for never having the money or time. Even if you are thinking or saying, "I wish I had the money to travel to some foreign place or take a cruise", you are focusing upon the fact that you now don't have enough. If you are constantly talking and think about not enough, you will likely never have enough.

Wishing is just that! It is a future hope, and as long as it is a future hope in your mind, it will remain a future hope in your reality. To realize your true desires, you must be constantly thinking and speaking with the expectation of your desires materializing in order to cause its manifestation. You have to *"reprogram"* your subconscious mind to expect to attain that which you desire.

When you look up "want" versus "expect" in the dictionary, you get very different meanings.

>Want: desire, wish for, fancy, crave, yearn for.

>Expect: wait for, anticipate, look forward to, count on, demand, insist on.

Think of the difference between a married couple who wants to have children, and a married couple who is expecting. How do they think about their future and how do they act? Your thoughts and actions about what you desire must be that distinctively different so that you expect what you desire.

"Next year I plan to travel to some foreign place or take a cruise." This is a much better thought than, "I wish I had the money to travel to some foreign place or take a cruise." The first way of expressing your desire shows your expectation of attaining your desire. Better yet, if you begin to gather the information about your trip, start planning what you'll do, and continue to think that somehow, some way, you know it will happen. Then the *Universal* **Law of Attraction** will set the forces in motion through the unlimited resources of the Universe in which your "I" is united, and the events that need to occur to deliver to you the circumstance of your true desire will manifest.

In order to change from wishful thinking that gets undesirable results, to manifestation or anticipative thinking, which brings about your true desires, you have to change the way you think and speak on an every day basis. Though you might not currently have the money or resources to achieve something you want to do, you can always speak and think in a way that attracts the money and resources to you. When you start to live life this way, everything you desire comes to you, and you are living the true nature of the **Law of Attraction**.

Now there is good news and bad news. The good news is that you already have the power and unlimited resources and you are already a master at using the **Law of Attraction**.

The bad news is, unfortunately, if you don't have what you desire in your life right now then you have been using this power to attract what you don't want.

The awesome news is that you can change that today by deciding to consciously direct the outcome of the **Law of Attraction**, instead of allowing it to work without your conscious input. Your past does not determine your future. However, your present thoughts that will. Again, it is not your past that determines your future; it is your current thoughts that determine your future.

Everything that manifests in your life is based on the **Law of Attraction**. If you are thinking poor, you are attracting poverty. If you are thinking rich, you are attracting wealth. If you are constantly thinking of being in trouble with the law, you attract lawlessness. If you believe that things never go your way, then you are inviting things to go wrong. Our world is exactly what we attract into it. You are right now attracting that which you believe you are worthy of, that which you believe you are capable of becoming, and that which your thoughts are focused upon.

In order to change your world, you first have to change your thoughts. If you will change your thoughts, everything will change for you. Thought is the seed of reality! Thought is what ultimately controls our destiny. When you control your thoughts, you shape your expectations and the realities of your expectations are delivered to you through the *Natural Laws* of the Universe.

Whether your thoughts are consciously being controlled to focus upon the expectation of that which you desire, or not, your thoughts will control your destiny every time. So the question is, do you want to control your destiny or not?

If you are not controlling your thoughts, you are not controlling your destiny and when you arrive at a destination, it will likely not be what you want it to be. However, whether you want it or not, your destination is always without fail a result of previous thoughts that you created and nourished. It's the result of what you convinced yourself to believe.

Fortune-tellers often have an impact on people's lives if what they say fits into the person's belief system. When a fortune-teller plants a thought into someone's mind, and that thought is something that the person really wants or believes, then the thought is nurtured and it will only be a matter of time before it manifests itself.

On the other hand, if the fortune-teller plants a thought that isn't something that the person really wants or believes, then the thought is discounted and believed to be untrue, and therefore not nurtured and will never manifest.

You can control the things that come into your life when you focus your attention on those thoughts that are in alignment with the true nature of your desires. Focusing only on thoughts of what you truly long for, emotionally, psychologically, intellectually and spiritually, with the expectation of success and you will cause those thoughts to become your reality.

How Do Negative Thoughts Affect Our Lives?

Unfortunately, there are people that go from one abusive relationship right into another. Why do you think that is so? Let's use an example: When one thinks thoughts of being needy they attract another who takes advantage of needy people. While they want something completely different, which is a loving and caring relationship, they get the exact opposite, because they think of themselves as needy. In order to attract a caring and loving relationship, they must first overcome thoughts of needing to be rescued, to thoughts of having something special to offer and understanding their true value as a person. This empowers them to attract a worthy companion that will be a loving and nurturing friend, lover and lifelong mate.

Many people have been brought up in homes that while having loving and caring parents or guardians to get them through the formative years, they also had a great deal of negative programming, which causes negative thinking and therefore negative results. It is not that they can't make it through life, because that is guaranteed. It is that they can't capitalize on every abundant resource that life has to offer because they don't know how to tap into these resources. It doesn't behoove anyone to go through life blaming anyone for his or her particular situation in life. It is up to everyone individually to take responsibility for their own lives and to make the necessary changes so that they can live a life that is completely functional, joyous, harmonious, and creates a life of abundant living.

None of us can change what has happened in our past, and it is our past and how we have thought in the past that has landed us where we are today. The awesome aspect of all of this is that we can control what is to be our destiny regardless of our past and we do that by starting today with our thoughts. Today's thoughts shape our expectations and what we become and therefore what we will attract in the future. If you want a destiny of abundance, prosperity and love, you begin by starting this very moment to nurture only those thoughts that will bring about the manifestation of those desires.

Notice we say, <u>this very moment</u>! This means that from this moment on, complaining about your status in life, your relationship with others, or any circumstance will only serve to continue its existence. Only by deciding to start from this moment on with thoughts and conversation about how your life is transformed and that everything you are attracting into your life are things that create more abundance, love and prosperity will you begin living an abundant life.

By starting right now to live the **Law of Attraction** with thoughts of drawing abundance, love and prosperity into your life, you will soon see the manifestation of such as your destiny unfolds. It will be no surprise to you when you get there because it will be exactly what you expect, nothing more and nothing less. You will become a magnet for everything you desire in life when your thoughts begin to bring forth feelings in you that create expectations, which will eventually manifest the reality of those things upon which you focused your thoughts. In other words, your thoughts of what you desire eventually become subconscious expectations and these empowering expectations will cause the manifestation of your desire every time.

MY THOUGHTS:

CHAPTER 3

"My Thoughts Control My Destiny - I Only Nurture Thoughts That Are In Accord With Harmonic Abundance"

"How does the Law of Attraction Work?"

There are Laws that the Universe responds to every time. The Universal Laws below are a few that make the **Law of Attraction** work.

> Law of Vibration
> Law of Reciprocity (or Love)
> Law of Fair Exchange
> Law of Growth

Let's start with the **Law of Vibration**, as this is an important principle in the **Law of Attraction**. Everything has a vibration. Vibration attracts like vibrations. When a certain key is hit on a piano it will make a crystal chandelier shake. The crystals in the chandelier have a vibration and the correct key on a piano that is in concert with that vibration makes the crystal shake. You want to be vibrating in harmony with those things you want to attract into your life. You can't attract the perfect companion if you are not the perfect companion for them. You both have to be vibrating at the same frequency. You can't attract prosperity and abundance if you are not in harmony with their vibrations either. It is our feelings that tell us if we are vibrationally aligned. If you have feelings on un-easiness you are not vibrationally aligned.

By nurturing thoughts of prosperity, which eventually will start to create feelings inside of you that are in harmony with prosperity, you will begin to attract all things prosperous into your life. Just like the **Law of Gravity**, if you fall, you will fall toward the earth, with the **Law of Attraction** when you are in the right vibration, you will attract what you desire into your life. Thus your outer world is determined by your inner world. You control your thoughts therefore you control your destiny.

Your destiny can now be one of prosperity, love and abundance because you now know the true essence of the **Law of Attraction**. Start today by nurturing thoughts of prosperity, love and abundance and the day will soon come that the manifestation of such will become your reality.

As a part of the unified Universe, we cannot provoke or alienate any other part of the Universe and gain personal benefit. However, the happiness, peace and harmony within the Universe depend upon the individual recognizing the interests of the Universe. So everything you think and do affects everyone and everything in the Universe. Everything is felt throughout the Universe to some degree, yet you will never personally benefit as a result of imposing harm to any part of the Universe. If you harm others, you harm the Universe and as part of the Universe, you harm yourself.

Conversely, if you do great things for others, you improve the Universe and as part of the Universe you will benefit.

This is one of the principles that you must focus upon, as well. The *Universal* **Law of Reciprocity**...the Universe will return to you that which you deliver to the Universe. With every thought, if you keep this in mind, you will change your thoughts to be constructive and you will not waste time or money on things that don't work within this principle. Many consider this the **Law of Love**. If you have unconditional love for everyone, you will give accordingly and therefore reap unconditional love in exchange.

The **Law of Fair Exchange** says that your result will be in direct proportion to your effort. This becomes a habit by practice. Repetition is the mother of skill. If you aren't already a master of correct, constructive thinking, now is the time to teach yourself. You will benefit from learning and integrating this principle in direct proportion to the effort you extend in learning it right now.

Here's where you can start.

>   I <u>can be</u> what I decide to be.
>   I <u>can be</u> what I desire to be.

I <u>can be</u> what I will to be.

Begin repeating these vision statements every morning and every night and multiple times throughout the day until it becomes a belief, while keeping in mind who and what the "I" really is. The spiritual "I" that understands that you cannot harm any other part of the Universe and benefit in any way.

Eventually, through repetition, this practice creates a new habit. Doing or saying something over and over until your subconscious has accepted it as a belief that you instinctively act upon creates habits. *"Sow a thought, reap and act, sow and act, reap a habit."*

You will begin to believe these statements and this belief will be instinctively acted upon. When you instinctively act upon these statements of belief, you will become invincible.

Do this…try to pick up an object near you. Were you able to pick it up? Of course you were. Trying is doing or not doing. You either picked up the object or you didn't, and whichever you did was your choice. That choice begins to create habits that will empower you or *dis*-empower you. Do not *try* to do anything. To quote Nike', "Just Do It." And if you're not going to just do it, then don't even try. Don't say you'll try when you know you have no intentions of following through. Try is simply failing with honor. The habit of failure is one of the most disempowering habits you can create. The mastery of abundant living requires that you replace thoughts of *"I'll try"* with thoughts and words of *"I will"*.

Below is the cycle of creating a new habit...

Unconsciously incompetent: We don't know what we don't know.
Consciously incompetent: We realize we don't know how to do it right.
Consciously competent: If we consciously think about it, we can do it right.
Unconsciously competent: We don't have to think about it and can do it right.

The unconsciously competent stage is when a new thought has become a habit and it becomes automatic. The subconscious mind considers it true and there is no longer any doubt about it.

Ensure that instead of living your life based on the habit of failure, that you create a new habit of success, which is a requirement to living in abundance. What is the success habit? It is ⟨ simple...do what you say you're going to Starting something with no intention of finishing it creates a habit of failure. Think about it. If you set goals that are achievable, and you simply don't follow through three out of four times, then you have created a belief that you fail at whatever you decide to accomplish. This is extremely disempowering. Jim Rohn, a business philosopher that Tammy respects immensely says, *"Something that is easy to do, is also easy not to do."* Don't get into the habit of not completing your easy predetermined goals even if it's easy to do. You create the habit of failure, instead of the habit of success.

When you decide, you must follow through because it is the lack of following through that creates the habit of failure. If this has been your past, change it today. Decide today you are going to repeat these vision statements mornings, evening, and several times throughout the day. Maybe at first you only want to commit to doing this for two weeks. Then after you've been successful accomplishing this two-week goal, then extend it two more weeks, and so on.

Once you have completed your commitment to yourself, you will have planted a seed of an empowering belief about your ability to be what you desire at will. You will also have created a success habit that will be so deep within your subconscious that when your goal is much larger, your subconscious will just kick in and execute based on your new habit of success.

Ultimately, do not say you'll "*try*" to do anything that you are capable of doing unless you are committed to following it through. Again, the words to use when undertaking any new endeavor or task is to say, "I *will* do it."

When you learn to simply do what you say you're going to do, not only will you gain credibility with everyone you encounter, but also you will find the power within the "I" that controls your outer world and your reality. The power within that will ultimately deliver to you in the outer world the evidence of your beliefs.

The first thing you must do in order to serve others is to make sure you have the wherewithal in this physical world in order to serve others. You cannot be generous to others unless you have abundance. You cannot give and serve others, unless you are strong. The "I" within you has access and the right to all of the abundance in the Universe in order to be strong to serve others. The "I" has access to all of the abundance and as long as you live within the "*Universal* **Law of Reciprocity**" or "**Law of Love**", what you desire is within your command and will be manifested to you.

The Infinite expresses and creates through the individual, and the individual expresses through the Universe or Infinite. When you are in alignment with all that is good, and being of service to the Universe, the Infinite united with the "I" within you sets the forces in motion so that the Infinite can create through you. Seek inspiration, and find the "I" within you.

Many people consider this "I" their spirit, soul, Holy Ghost or their connection with God. In any case, when your soul is dead, life ceases to exist. It is your spiritual connections that will assist you in attracting abundance, and will work to deliver to you the evidence of your beliefs. It is your realization and acknowledgement that God is within you, and that is what will allow you access to life's abundance.

If you recall, the cause behind all effects is within or that "I" within you. Your Spirit is the part of you that is part of the Infinite. It is the part of you that is the Creator within your conscious influence. It is most important for you to come into realization of your conscious power. As a recap, your conscious thoughts create your habits and beliefs. It creates your awareness of who you are, or your awareness of being. So it is crucial for you to understand your conscious power.

Power comes through tranquility…seek silence and stillness often because if you quite your mind and body, you can think correctly and it is thought that is the secret to creativity and ultimately your ability to manifest your desires.

The **Law of Vibration** carries light and electricity. We know it works, even though we don't see it.

Thought, similarly, is carried through the **Law of Vibration**. So thought vibrates beyond our physical being and unites with the Infinite.

Now consider the **Law of Love**. Love is in direct alignment with the Infinite, so thoughts based in Love are given vitality through the "I" that is united with the Infinite.

It's the **Law of Growth** in which thoughts take form and expression. It is the emotions that give feeling to thoughts so that thoughts will take form. If you have a thought that is based upon the **Law of Love**, it is in direct alignment with the Infinite and is united with the Infinite through the "I" within you and takes form through the **Law of Growth**.

How do we develop the faith, courage and passion, which will accomplish this chain of events that will ultimately deliver to you the expression of your thoughts and desires? Practice and repetition! Not the practice of negative behaviors, but rather the practice of perfect behaviors. *"Perfect practice makes perfect"*. When we practice perfect principles based on the *Laws of the Universe*, the manifestations of those perfect practices are always in line with what we desire.

Many people think about acquiring things for selfish reasons. The more you think about serving others, and you realize that selfish thoughts are the poison that will kill any positive growth, the more you will come to know the true power of your thoughts. The more we serve, the more we will receive. *"Sow abundance, reap abundance!"*

MY THOUGHTS:

MY THOUGHTS:

Chapter 4

"I Release Any and All Barriers Both Conscious and Un-Conscious To My Personal and Financial Success!"

The **Law of Attraction** will draw to us that which is most predominant in our mind. If your predominant thought is constructive and harmonious, the result will be constructive; if your thought is destructive or discordant, the result will be destructive. This could possibly be the origin of good and evil. Good, being that of love for all, and fear being our personal devil. Fear can be hate, guilt, worry, anxiety, or many other emotions that don't feel very good and ultimately relate back to some form or fear.

Fear will always take us away from the things we want and love and faith will always take us toward the things we want. The **Law of Attraction** simply will not let two conflicting ideas come together. If you desire something yet fear aspects of what that desire entails, you will simply be keeping your desire away from you.

To illustrate, let's say you want to be a singer, but you have a fear of being in front of people. The **Law of Attraction** will keep you from your desire because you will have attracted an environment, which would not include singing in front of people. The desire can never be attained if in any way, fear is attached to its attainment. As long as you maintain the fear, the thing you want most will elude you.

Your thoughts control your destiny, and you control your thoughts therefore you control your destiny. Do you want to be a singer? Simply release the fear and the avenues to becoming a singer will open up for you. As long as you hold onto fear, you give up the destiny of becoming a singer.

No matter what your desire is the **Law of Attraction** is always working. The **Law of Attraction** is working to protect you from pain or help move you closer to those things that give you pleasure. In order to capitalize on the law, you must understand the nature of the law and how to work within its precepts.

> *"In Santa Monica there was a 12-year-old girl that was there to sing with a Church group that was performing on Third Street commonly known as "The Promenade". When this young girl got up to sing, she suddenly froze, began to cry, and ran over to her mother. The two of them were only a few feet from me so I spoke to the girl's mother and told her that I could help her daughter overcome the fear. The mother agreed to allow me to do this. In less then two minutes the little girl ran back over to the person leading the group and told him she wanted to sing. When the band finished the song they were performing, the young girl went to*

the microphone and without hesitation sang her song." ~Bruce Goldwell

Releasing fear can be instantaneous or it can take time. The choice is really up to each individual. You must keep in mind that the **Law of Attraction** works every time, without fail 24 hours a day, 7 days a week, and 365 days a year. No exceptions! As long as you hold on to fear, it will always be keeping you from the things you want in life.

Think of a dark room with no light in it. When you hold onto fear, there is no light in the room. When you turn on a light, the darkness is gone. You can get rid of fear by replacing it with something else. When you replace thoughts of fear, lack and limitation with thoughts of courage, power, self-reliance and confidence your mental and spiritual world around you will change.

Since fear is responsible for all negative emotions release or replace fear, and all associated feelings with those of love and all its associated feelings then your reality will change significantly.

> Fear – Courage
> Lack – Abundance
> Illness – Health

For every fearful feeling there is an offsetting pleasurable feeling that we desire. Release fearful feeling by replacing your thoughts with the offsetting pleasurable feeling. These pleasurable feelings always have love as a foundation. Once you learn to live in *love mode*, you will be attracting those things that you desire and the Universe will be the instrument that rushes them to you.

In order to change the *"world-without"* we must change the *"world-within"*. By getting rid of fear from your inner world, you immediately change your outer world and begin to experience those things that come to those who vibrate in the realm of love. The kind of friends that you make will be more loving, the relationships you have will be more loving, and all business and personal relationships will be those whose vibrations are love. You will be able to tell the difference between the two. You will instinctively stay away from those people who are not conducive to the new vibration you are living.

Everyone seeks after three basic things in life: Health, Wealth and Love. Of these three, love is the one thing that affects all other things in our lives. When we don't feel love, we can suffer poor health and it might even affect our performance at work, which can affect the incomes we receive. It also affects our ability to have trusting relationships, which will affect our ability to earn, because in all financial ventures trusting relationships are crucial.

When we increase the love in our life, all other things can also increase as well as our health and our abundance.

We feel love in two ways: Love from others and love of self. By first loving yourself, we open up the door to feel more love from others. By loving yourself, you also have the capacity to love others more. Getting rid of fear allows us to love our self as well as others more abundantly.

So how can you eliminate fear immediately upon beginning to feel it?

Remember the young girl who was afraid of singing in front of the large crowd yet she was *immediately* transformed and overcame her fear? She was asked a few simple questions which she answered without hesitation, then she exercised a simple process, which allowed her to release her fear. Most people are able to do this simple exercise and get rid of their fears immediately.

Here are the questions the young girl was asked:

> Do you like that feeling?
> Do you want to get rid of it?
> Are you willing to get rid of it?
> When?

The answer to the first question is without hesitation always answered by people with a resounding "No" which is always the case with the second question as well. Asking the question, "Are you willing to get rid of it?" is sometimes answered with hesitation. It is not hesitation due to the fact that people aren't *willing* to release their fear; it is more because they are not sure how they are going to "Will" it.

"*Will*" is the one predominant factor that determines your success in any venture or undertaking. Where there is a "*Will*" there is a way! If you "*Will*" something strong enough, you can accomplish anything and success will always be imminent.

Once you have decided that you are *willing* to give up your fear then the last question, which is also very important, is "When?" It is the "When" that allows you to change your life immediately or sometime in the future. Allowing the **Law of Attraction** to continue to keep you from those things you desire is simply a choice. You choose when you want to allow the **Law of Attraction** to bring your most precious desires into your life or to hold them at bay. You yourself are the *Master* of your universe and only you. No one else can make these choices for you. It is only you!

So it is with this understanding that you are offered these solutions to releasing your fear so that the room in which you reside is of the light and not of darkness. Once you are in the light, or in other words living the Laws of *Love*, *Abundance* and all other *Laws of the Universe* that will bring about *Health*, *Wealth and Love* into you life, the **Law of Attraction** will guarantee the manifestation of the things that you desire.

Once you have answered the four questions above with the appropriate answers, you can do this exercise, which will release the fear according to your *"Will"*. Close your eyes and take a deep breathe. Begin to think about your fear and count slowly from one to three. When you get to three, release the breath and imagine, as you blow the air out that the fear is also leaving along with the breath. Open your eyes and take a deep breathe imagining as you draw in the air that light and love is now filling your lunges as well as your body and mind.

Allow love as well as thoughts of power, strength, courage and self-confidence and all other positive emotions to be the predominant feelings in your life. By controlling your thoughts and what you allow yourself to hold onto, you control the very things that come into your life on a daily basis.

There will be some who after doing this exercise have such strong ties to their fears that they just cannot *"will"* them away. There is a solution for all problems and everyone has a way to achieve all things in life. There is no vacancy in the Universe. For those who are able to release fear immediately, they can immediately replace fear with other thoughts and feelings that are of a positive nature. On the other hand, for those who cannot create the vacancy that needs to be filled, the answer is to change the darkness to light by simply filling the room with light whereby there is no room for darkness.

To do this, you must completely fill your mind with positive affirmations pushing out the negative thoughts. With new positive thoughts constantly filling your mind, it is only a matter of time before the old negative thoughts will have no power over you and you will find yourself drawing the things into your life that you have desired. The transition from living in lack, fear, frustration, discord and doubt to living a life of abundance, prosperity, confidence and love will be forthcoming. Keep in mind that a positive thought is *one hundred times* stronger then a negative one, because positive thoughts are in alignment with the Infinite and draws upon the power of the *Universe*. Negative thoughts are not in alignment with the Infinite and simple stays with you until you do something about them.

One of the important keys to achieving all of the abundance the Universe has available for you is *"Will"*. If you lack the *"Will"* to find the time to use affirmations that will transform your life, then you <u>will not</u> achieve the desired result, which is the manifestation of your dreams. Simply plant a seed and watch it grow. A statement as simple as, "I *will* be what I *will* to be" can begin to transform you to a higher level of reality and impress upon you the idea that if something as simple as this can begin the transformation, what can others of like nature achieve?

> *"Everyday in every way, I am getting better and better."*

> *"My thoughts control my destiny, therefore I control my thoughts"*

> *"Everyone and everything that will help me accomplish my dreams is coming into my life now."*

The mastery of abundant living is achievable by everyone. There is no lack in the Universe. It is filled with abundance. As you fill your thoughts with thoughts of abundance, hope, love, prosperity and plenty, your life will be filled with abundance, hope, love, prosperity and every other needful thing.

How can you achieve this?

There are literally hundreds of thousand of affirmations or vision statements that can be written to cover any and all circumstances in life. While anyone and everyone can use these vision statements, some of the most useful declarations are the ones you can create for yourself. It doesn't take a rocket scientist to write an affirmation that will affect your life in a profound way. It is simply a matter of figuring out what the predominant things are that keep you from your dreams and desires and turning them around so that they are the assets that get you there.

What do you believe is the predominant thing that is keeping you from that which you most desire? Is it the lack of money? Is it not enough time? Is it the absence of appropriate relationships? All of these things are basically a fear of not having enough of something. So it is essential to turn these thoughts into more empowering thoughts of love and abundance. Let's use lack of money as an example. . You may have at times thought to yourself, "*I'd really like to do that, but I don't have the money!*" Rather then thinking or saying, "*I don't have the money*" respond with thoughts that are more empowering based in love and abundance.

> "*I have all the money I need to accomplish my dreams and goals.*"
>
> "*I'm so grateful for finding the path that is continuing to lead me to financial freedom.*"
>
> "*I make excellent money decisions.*"
>
> "*When I decide not to do something that cost money, it's because I have chosen to invest my money more wisely and in a way that will pay back to me a greater return.*"

Keeping in mind that a positive affirmation that is in vibrational alignment with the Universe is *one hundred times* stronger then a negative one, what do you think would be the outcome of any of the statements above as apposed to the first statement focusing on the lack of money?

Write down every thing you can think of that is keeping you from your dreams. Make a list of as many as you can so that you can re-write them into positive affirmations that will transform you from lack to plenty.

> Negative - *"I would like to be a singer but I am afraid of singing in front of people."*
>
> Positive – *"I am confident and strong and feel comfortable when I sing in front of others."*

When a negative thought comes into your mind, that of anger, lack, doubt, worry, guilt or any fear based negative thought, immediately replace them with one or more of your affirmations or vision statements that empower you and attract more of what you want into your life. The way to fight darkness is with light; we fight the cold with heat and we fight every evil with good. Denials and negative thoughts never created any success. Affirm only that which is positive and good and your life will be filled with such. That which is bad will vanish from your life without incident.

MY THOUGHTS:

CHAPTER 5

"When I Create Ideal Visions And Rehearse My Future, I Am Presented With Ideal Opportunities That Match My Intention."

The **Law of Attraction** is working at all times in your life whether you are aware of it or not. The principles that comprise the law are easy to understand and use. The more proficient we become with the principles the more we will accelerate the process of the manifestation of those things we desire. Our current reality is a result of past thoughts and our current thoughts are the seeds upon which our future reality originates. By learning the principles and practicing, we empower ourselves to have more abundance, more wealth, more love and more happiness in our lives.

If there is one principle that's considered to be the most crucial in *"Mastering"* the **Law of Attraction**, it is the ability to imagine creatively in your minds eye. When you can see what you desire in your minds eye with the intensity, clarity and passion that utilizes all of your senses, its manifestation not only eminent but can be accelerated.

It is that first thought that begins the creative process, it is the nurturing of the thought, through creative visualization, that brings it to reality. *"Sew a thought, reap an act..."* This process works every time without fail. Look at what is being manifest in your life right now. Is everything that is in your life at this very moment what you really want or are the things in your life those things that you most think about and talk about? If the things you are experiencing in your life are things you really don't want rather then the things you really desire, then it is time to examine your daily activities, thoughts and conversations.

If you want to change your life, you have to change your predominant thoughts and conversations. What is really awesome about the **Law of Attraction** is the immediacy in how it reacts to what we are doing, saying, thinking and our actions. By focusing your thoughts on what you desire and speaking and acting consistently with those thoughts, you ensure that the outcome of the creative process is exactly what you desired it to be.

The subconscious mind is extremely powerful. It doesn't "think" it just does what it's been taught to do. It doesn't know the difference between fiction and reality. So if we train our subconscious by showing it the perfect picture of our desired reality, it will act as if it's true and set the forces in motion to deliver us that which we desire.

To help understand how you can focus your thoughts so that your creative process attracts what you really intend, Bruce Goldwell shares the following example:

> "When I began writing the book 'Dragon Keepers', I closed my eyes several times a day and began imaging the following."
>
> "I would see myself at one of the awards ceremonies for the movies. I saw the celebrities, producers and others sitting around me in their tuxedos and the ladies in their beautiful gowns. I could smell the perfume in the air around me. The people were all talking among each other and shaking hands and wishing each other well. The lights in the auditorium lit the room up and everything was spectacular. I would see, smell, hear, touch and even taste anything I could there in my imagination.
>
> The lights went dim and a hush came over the room. Then the music began to play and performers came on stage with the lights shining on them. Energy filled the room like nothing I have ever felt before. As the ceremony progressed a card is pulled from an envelope and the announcement is made; "Dragon Keepers is the winner." I jump up from my seat, as do others who helped in the process of creating the movie. We get on stage and are handed the awards. Each takes their turn at the podium.

> *When I get up to the microphone, I thank all my fans, the people who supported the making of the movie and all those who watched it on screen. I thank those people especially who purchased the book, which made it a best seller, which in turn created the need to make a movie.*
>
> *As I leave the stage with the others, I see and hear the people in the audience again applauding offering their love and support. It is an awesome experience."*

As you can see from the example, every aspect of the experience was imagined in the mind using all the senses to visualize the experience. What has been the outcome of this particular visualization thus far? A publisher was acquired before the book was completed, a Co-producer agreed to be part of the movie production, and an FX producer from a well known movie sent an email to the author requesting to be notified when the movie is in production so they can be a part of it. That is not the whole of it, however enough to help you understand that the creative process immediately manifested certain things required to bring about the end result. All of this occurred prior to the book being completed and ready to be published.

The Universe will correspond to the nature of your desire and begin manifesting its reality immediately. Everything will come forth in its own due time and always in concert with what is required to bring about the reality of your desire. Using your imagination to begin the creative process of bringing your thoughts into reality is essential to your success.

> *"Imagination is the beginning of creation. You imagine what you desire, you will what you imagine and at last you create what you will."*
> ~George Bernard Shaw

You must have a clear, vivid picture of the desired result as you wish it to be. You must savor in the feelings of enjoying your life this way. You must imagine that you have already achieved it and are now living it.

Not only does imagining things from this perspective allow you to understand what is to become of your future, but you will develop faith, confidence, endurance, courage and enthusiasm for your desires. You will develop a passion for your desires, and for life.

So…what are your dreams?

You can begin right now to use the creative process to set in motion the **Law of Attraction** so your dreams will become your future reality. *"If it's to be, it's up to me."* You are the one who controls what your future has in store for you.

It is a simple process and with time, you will become more and more proficient at it. Don't worry if you don't see every detail. What is important is that your thought process allows you to think of as many details as possible. Each time you can build upon the scenario of your dream. The manifestation of what you imagine will always be more exciting when you get there then what you might possibly dream up in your mind yet it will always be in line with what you desired.

There is one additional step that would be suggested based on feedback from those who have implemented it. Replay your perfect mental visualization backwards in your mind. In other words, when you have created that future event and see it in your mind and have examined as many details of it as possible, ask yourself how you got to that point.

Let's refer to the example given earlier regarding the Dragon Keepers movie and award.

How did this award ceremony come to be? Tens of thousands and even millions of people watched the movie and it got many outstanding reviews.

How did that happen? The movie was produced and released to movie theaters for public viewing.

And how did it get there? The book became a *Best Seller* as tens of thousands of people purchased the book from stores as well as the Internet.

I like to tell people that they are creating a video of their perfect reality in reverse while winding the reel so that it can be played out in real life. It shouldn't include every aspect of what will occur in the process, as the Universe with its unlimited resources knows better how to fill in the blanks. However, it is nice to have some key elements of what the creative process will unfold so that you recognize the road marks when you get there.

Have fun with this process. This is your chance to let your imagination fly. Maybe that student who you thought was just daydreaming in the classroom is the one who is using something that the Universe intended for all of us to use in our lives, the creative visualization of our future reality. Wouldn't it be nice if in our educational system they taught people how to think and how to create…*how to dream perfect dreams?*

Go ahead! Find a quiet spot at home, outside near water, on a mountain or any place among nature. All these are wonderful places to dream. Wherever you typically meditate and let your imagination soar or simply close your eyes on that trip home on the bus from work. What is most important is that you are taking time out each day to dream of what you want and see it in your mind as already existing. The day will soon come when the manifestation of that dream *will* occur.

MY THOUGHTS:

CHAPTER 6

"I Allow The Possibilities To Unfold Before Me And Am Inspired Down The Right Path"

We have examined the fact that our thoughts determine our future and that the Universe manifest those thoughts that are most predominant. As we understand this concept and begin to focus on those things we desire the most, it now becomes important to be aware of the things that are presented to you either through inspired thought or the opportunities that become manifest in your life.

Almost every minute of every day we are presented with options and opportunities. As you focus on the things you want, opportunities that will deliver you your desires will start to unfold before you. When these possibilities present themselves, it is up to you to act. Your actions, or lack there of, will determine the path you will take.

The Universe has infinite resources and therefore, there are multiple ways that your desires can be delivered, and you may be presented with a possibility that is completely different than what you had in mind. Approaching everything with a detachment to a predetermined path keeps you open to recognize possibilities as they are presented.

Try this exercise and don't look ahead!

1. For about ten seconds, look around the room and try to find everything in the room that's red. Then close your eyes for about ten seconds and remember everything you saw that was red. When you open your eyes, go to step two.

2. Now remember everything that was red. Can you see it in your minds eye even thought your eyes are open? Now without looking around in the room, name everything you saw that was green. Can you remember anything?

Chances are you remembered more red things than green things. When you are focused on a predetermined path, you are not as open to seeing other possibilities. Make sure that you aren't so focused on a specific path that you miss a better opportunity.

Additionally, because the Universe has unlimited resources, you may be given multiple opportunities and have to choose. If you make choices based on a consensus of having asked many others what they would do, the choice you make is still your choice and all the responsibility of those choices is yours and yours alone.

So how can you be sure that the path you choose is the right one?

This is where your feelings come into play. When you feel good about a decision then it is highly probable that it is a good choice. But if somewhere in your gut, something doesn't feel right then it is probably a decision that will take you further away from your desire.

Most often, however, you should follow your inspiration. Making a decision based on what others prefer should not be done especially when it goes against your intuition. You don't drive a car down the road allowing others to steer it for you. The same is true with your life. You want to go through life being the person who chooses what you "*will*" do.

The "I" within you has all the resources needed to accomplish anything that you want or desire. As this inner voice becomes more in touch with the *Universe* you will be more attune to the inspirations that the Universe offers you. The more you detach yourself from a predetermined path and *"allow"* your feelings to be the monitor, the easier it is to stay in harmony with the Universe, and it is in harmony where your desires will be manifested with absolute precision.

It might take a little bit of soul searching to find the mindset that is needed in order to be prepared for what the Universe is willing to manifest into your life. The "*allowing*" that is required in order to receive any desire must be unambiguous. You cannot want something and not want something. You can't desire something and yet not be sure you are really ready for it.

By "*allowing*" all possibilities to unfold before you and "*allowing*" yourself to be inspired down the right path, you can be led directly and most assuredly to that thing you desire. No one walks through a closed door. Insure that your "*allowing*" is without doubt, without hesitation and without reservations.

When an opportunity presents itself and it feels right, then act, act precisely, act immediately and act unequivocally. Be fully prepared to receive that which you desire and know that the "I" within you is connected to the Universe in such a way that nothing, absolutely nothing that you intend, which is good and in harmony with the Universe, will ever fail to be manifest into your life.

An example of how "*intending*" and "*allowing*" works, we share with you how this book came to be.

> *Bruce Goldwell decided to write a book with the title "Mastery of Abundant Living". The purpose of the book is evident in what has been said throughout it.*
>
> *As Bruce pondered writing this book, he decided*

*that it would be best to have a co-writer. He thought that idea over for a couple of days and then he came across someone while surfing online who moderated a group that was studying the Universal Laws. You guessed it! Tammy Lynch is that moderator. It was clear that Tammy had a perspective of the **Law of Attraction** that would compliment Bruce's thoughts, ideas, knowledge and feelings. He sent an email introducing himself and let her know about his plan to write this book.*

*One of his first emails to her said, "I feel inspired to ask you something. I am planning to write a book called 'Mastery of Abundant Living'. It is based on the **Law of Attraction** and how others can master this process. I feel that I need to ask you if you would like to co-write this book with me."*

The response that Bruce got was direct and to the point. Tammy wrote, "Based on what I am currently doing, I feel that I am supposed to write this book with you. Let's talk about it."

As you can see, both Tammy and Bruce were *"allowing"* all possibilities to unfold before them and they were feeling that what was being proposed was the right thing to do. By being open to their *"allowing"* and *"receiving"*, they worked in harmony with the Universe and the book unfolded and became manifest with exact precision.

The **Law of Attraction** works every time, without fail, guaranteed! Every time you manifest a dream or desire, you can build bigger and better dreams. There is no limit to what you can do. Dream big! Dream often! Allow all possibilities to unfold before you and be inspired down the right path. The Universe is on your side every second, of every minute, of every day.

MY THOUGHTS:

CHAPTER 7

"How do I Apply the Law of Attraction"

By now, you must realize that the Universe has Unlimited resources and everything in abundance, and our natural state of being is perfect, strong, powerful, loving and harmonious.

So how do we become a *Master of Abundant Living*?

Let's review the principles we've covered so far and apply it to abundant *Health*, *Wealth* and *Love*.

- All Power Comes from Within
- Control Your Thoughts
- Use Vision Statements
- Visualization (Create-a-Vision)
- Allow for all Possibilities

<u>All Power Comes From Within</u>

It's necessary to understand that all power comes from within and the "I" within you is spiritual with *unlimited power and resources*. Most people only live in their physical or outer world, yet it is the "I" within you that creates everything in the outer world through its unlimited resources in which you have access to in your inner world.

Our natural state of being is perfect, strong, powerful, loving and harmonious, and it is when we are a vibrational match to this state, that every cell in our body thrives, and the vibration that permeates the Universe is a vibrational match to the Infinite.

Have faith that whatever you can become in your imagination, with conviction, you can realize in the outer world.

Control Your Thoughts

Consciously control your thoughts and become a dreamer. Throw away your limitations and allow your thoughts to shape your beliefs in perfect idealism. Feel what it's like to be whom you desire. These perfect inner thoughts and feelings become your beliefs and personal truths. Once your thought becomes your truth, it becomes part of your instinctive nature and through the *All Powerful* "I" within you; you draw to you those things that match your belief.

Your unity with everything and everyone is "*All Powerful*" and always present, whether you realize it or not. Every thought, therefore, is the cause of a reaction. You think something with enough concentration, and it becomes true for you in your inner world and correlates with matching things in your outer world.

There will always be a reaction to your thoughts *every time*! It actually is the only way anything in your outer world is created. All power is under your control through your thoughts and beliefs through your unity with the Infinite.

In whatever you desire, you are to ensure that disempowering thoughts are eliminated, and your ideal perfection remains as your focus. You begin to consciously think empowering thoughts consistent with your desires and you begin to feel the joy associated with already being there.

Use Vision Statements

You immediately implement a routine that includes speaking, thinking and writing down affirmations, or statements of your vision. You do this multiple times in a day. Start and end your day with perfect vision statements. Add them to your daily meditation. Additionally, simultaneously you must ensure that disempowering thoughts don't get access to your mind. Turn on your SPAM blocker, and keep the *"stinking thinking"* out of your head.

When a disempowering thought enters your mind, your objective is to get it out immediately. Breathe deep, and substitute the thought for one that is more empowering. Feel the way you'd feel if your desire were your reality.

Visualization (Create-a-Vision)

Visualization is essential to manifesting your desires. It is *"The Secret"*. What will manifest in the outer world must first be created in your imagination.

Visualize the perfect image of your desire. Dream it; feel it; and hold the image in your mind's eye. Feel the way it feels. The rest will unfold and the details will develop, as you are led to your desires. Keep the ideal image without conditions or limitations. Make it perfect to you. Visualize others responding the way that you desire. See yourself as the best of what you desire.

Do this daily. Repetition of a thought or feeling is what creates the belief. Your subconscious doesn't know the difference between your imagination and your reality, and since pleasurable thoughts expand at a rapid pace due to their alignment with the Universe, you will soon be seeing the evidence of your desire develop in your outer world.

Allow for the Best Outcome

You will be given opportunities that will expand and develop into that which you desire. You will be inspired to take a path at precisely the right time that will result in the right effect. Detach yourself from the outcome and be open to the possibilities that are presented to you. Don't predetermine the path as you may miss the perfect opportunity being presented. The finite beings that we are can't possibly predetermine a path that is as powerful as the Infinite, so don't close your mind to Infinite possibilities that may be presented.

Allow the possibilities to unfold and take action when they present themselves. Don't doubt this process; just open yourself up to the *Unlimited Power* that will deliver to you everything you desire.

MY THOUGHTS:

CHAPTER 8

A Guide to Meditation

If you've never meditated before you might wonder "what's the benefit?" Why would you spend 15 to 30 minutes a day doing nothing?

There are two major benefits. First, the easiest way that we have found to describe this benefit is to compare meditation to re-booting a computer. Think of your computer running multiple programs and processes. It gets locked up because there's so much going on that its memory can't handle it. So you re-boot your computer, and then it begins to work again the way it was mean to work.

When your mind has multiple processes working all at once, and you are stressed, have anxiety, or have negative feelings of any sort, you don't think clearly. The solar plexus, the brain of the subconscious mind, contracts giving less energy to all of the cells in your body, which can result in many ills or stresses of the body. Your conscious and subconscious minds have difficulty getting what they need in order to operate with clarity and efficiency.

Meditation, similar to re-booting a computer, shuts down all of the processes except for the vitals, allowing your solar plexus to expand and radiate energy to every part of the body. You develop clarity of thought and amazingly enough, with time and practice, creative, inspired thought is usually the result, which is the second benefit.

It is in silence that you come in contact with the Divine. Power comes through tranquility…seek silence and stillness often because if you quite your mind and body, you can think correctly and it is thought that is the secret to creativity and ultimately your ability to manifest your desires.

Meditation, to be effective, will require practice. If you haven't meditated before, each step below should be repeated a minimum of three to four days or preferably every day for a week, or until you've mastered each step. Master each step prior to progressing to the next. Commit 15 to 30 minutes per day every day.

The first step to meditation is to learn how to control your physical body.

Select a room where you can be alone and undisturbed, and that is available daily. This is the location you should meditate whenever possible. The methods that we are providing are more contemporary and may not follow other traditional methods. However, we have found them to be more universally accepted and comfortable.

Traditionally, the proper position in which to meditate is sitting erect with your legs crossed. Some will take their feet and place them on top of their calves versus underneath, either one foot or both.

There are a couple different philosophies in regards to hand position, but the ultimate goal is to stay still and to relax and do not clench your hands.

Instead of sitting, it is becoming more common to lie on your back with your hands flat on your sides. This is more comfortable for most and allows a deeper physical relaxation for novice meditators. In either position, keep your head in alignment so that your spine through your neck is level.

Do not have any noise in the background, including music. Let your thoughts roam where they will but be perfectly still for a minimum of fifteen minutes to half an hour; continue this for a minimum of three to four days or until you secure full control of your physical being. You must master securing control of your physical being before progressing to the next step.

Once you have mastered securing control of your physical body, then you're going to progress to controlling your thoughts.

In your meditation room, in your preferred position, continue to be perfectly still, then begin to stop all thought. When you have a thought pop into your head, clear it immediately.

This is easier said than done. If you struggle eliminating thought we have a couple options for you.

Begin to focus upon your breathing, so your only thought is on your breathing. When you inhale, feel the oxygen enter your body and instantly give healthy energy to all of your cells in your body. Upon exhaling, feel the thought leave your mind as the air leaves your body taking with it the thought and any impurities in your body.

Another option is to simply count every time you inhale and every time you exhale. As a new thought enters your mind, refocus on your counting with each inhale and exhale.

You may also try concentrating on feeling the pulse in your big toes one foot at a time. Once you feel it, stay focused on the pulse. If a new thought pops into your mind, move to your heels and again try to find and feel your pulse and stay focused on the pulse.

Again, if a new thought enters your mind, move to your knees and continue this process on multiple parts of your body every time a new thought enters your mind. You will find fewer interruptions of thought as you progress up the body.

Being able to hinder thoughts will ultimately give you control over all thoughts and will enable you to direct your thoughts to only those you desire. Continue this for three or four days or until you are able to hinder your thoughts.

Now that you've mastered controlling your physical body, and inhibiting thought, we will take it one step further. Remain still and inhibit all thought, and begin to relax every muscle and nerve in your body, release all tension.

Physical relaxation is a learned behavior and enables the blood to circulate freely through out your body to and from the brain. Physical tightness leads to irregular mental activity or restless mind syndrome and results in the lack of clarity.

If you find this difficult, use the method of feeling your pulse and as you move your concentration from your toes up your body to one body part at a time, relax the muscles around the pulse that you're focusing upon.

Continue this until you feel still, quite, relaxed, restful and at peace with yourself and the world.

Next, it's time to mentally relax and let go of all stress and all negative feelings and thoughts. As always, don't progress unless you have mastered control of your thoughts and body, and are able to physically relax every muscle and nerve in your body.

You mentally relax by letting go of all adverse conditions including hatred, anger, worry, jealousy, envy, sorrow, trouble, disappointment or fear of any kind.

Don't let your emotions control you. Instead, allow your intellect to take over and control your emotions. Release all negativity. You can let go. And once you do you will experience mental freedom, and the subconscious mind will begin to operate from a fresh new day. The solar plexus will begin to operate instinctively.

Mental freedom is the first step in allowing you to consciously direct your use of the **Law of Attraction**. Once you have mastered this, your body and mind will no longer control you. In fact, it is your body and mind that will become a slave to you; the "I" within you will be the Master.

The final step to meditation is your imagination. This is where you create the perfect image of your desires. Make a complete mental picture of it, see the buildings, the grounds, the trees, friends, associations, everything complete. It's likely at first, that you will find yourself thinking of everything under the sun, except your perfect ideal. That's okay, but remember to eliminate any unwanted thought. Ultimately, you want your imagination to be consciously creating the perfect result of your desire. Concentrate your focus upon your ideal, limitless, fantasy of what you are to become and enjoy the pleasures of your accomplishments.

Focus upon the end result desired, not how you get there, or the lack thereof. If you are looking to improve your health, see yourself as vibrant and cured; if you desire financial wealth, see yourself in your new home; if it's the ideal relationship you're yearning for, imagine your life partner and every desirable trait they possess.

MY THOUGHTS:

MY THOUGHTS:

CHAPTER 9

"Creating Abundant Health"

Every cell in your body is intelligent and knows exactly what to do to survive and be healthy. Each cell acts to benefit the overall good of the whole. When you don't let your light shine you bring about discord and disease. When you live in your natural state of being, your cells are provided with the energy needed to survive and thrive and to attain their healthy state.

Your physical health today is a result of your past beliefs, which were created by your thoughts and feelings. Your behavior of the recent past is a reflection of your beliefs, which are a result of your past thoughts and feelings. Ultimately your past thoughts and feelings created the chain of events that resulted in your current physical health.

However, if you decide today that you are going to change your current physical health and you know that success is guaranteed then you will immediately begin to change your thoughts. The changes will include how you think about your food intake and exercise among other things. Your beliefs know that improvements in this regard will result in improved health and attaining your ideal weight.

Ask yourself *"what does someone with great health do differently than I?"* If you truly know you'll attain your perfect health, then you must begin to think, feel and act as someone in perfect health. As long as you believe you will achieve it, then subconsciously you will begin doing what people in perfect health do.

To get started, you must first decide to change your behavior. The mind and body cannot be separate. For example, if you behave like you are already your ideal weight, and in perfect health, your subconscious will believe it to be true, and you can therefore begin attracting what you need to manifest it into reality.

Hypothetically, if you weigh 200 lbs and desire to be 130 lbs, and you begin to act and feel like you're 130 lbs, you will become 130 lbs eventually. Mind and body are connected and it's impossible for them to have opposing beliefs and ultimately opposing outcomes.

Tom Hopkins, in the "Official Guide to Success" says, *"Fake it, until you make it."* If you act like you're already where you want to be, the belief and physical reality will follow. Neville in his book "At Your Command" says *"you must shut the door on that which you are now aware of being, and rise in consciousness to that which you desire to be."*

Let's review the steps…

All Power Comes from Within: Remember that all power comes from within and that the Infinite Power within will attract what you need in order to attain your ideal health.

Control Your Thoughts: You must control your thoughts and ensure that thoughts of health are always commanding the desired health.

Vision Statements: Begin to create new beliefs by thinking, saying and writing vision statements affirming what you desire, as if you have already attained it.

Create-a-Vision: You must create the vision in your minds eye of what you desire your health to be, with colors and feeling and smells.

Allow for the Best Outcome: With a consistent focus you will attract or draw to you what you need to manifest perfect health into your reality. You will be presented with options that will guide you to your ideal health

All Power Comes From Within

It is essential that you have advanced in your understanding that all power comes from within. Without this recognition, you can easily find reasons to blame something other than yourself for any circumstance you may have with your current physical health.

We realize that issues associated with your current physical health may have begun due to something beyond your control, such as heredity, or a medical situation. However, it is within your control to change it. Until you recognize this to be true, you may continue to blame some circumstance that you believe is outside of your control for where you're at today and this ultimately, will keep you right where you are today.

Your expectations in life, whether desired or not, are shaped by your beliefs, and your beliefs are a product of your conscious thought. If God, or whomever you call your Higher Power, is within you, and you are made in His image and likeness, then His power is within you. Do you believe that God has the Power to cure whatever your ill may be? Do you think that your Higher Power has the resources to find a way to guide you to your ideal health and weight?

The Infinite creates through the individual. Therefore if your Higher Power has the power and resources to guide you to ideal health, and He creates through the individual, then it is you that has His power.

However, none of this works if you don't believe

you have this Power. You do have the Power. It lies within you. It is the "I" within you that is united with the Infinite resources of your Higher Power, which will ensure your successful result, if you believe.

If you don't believe that you have the Power, and you believe that Infinite does not have the Power to deliver anything that is for your good to you, then your weight loss, or health improvement, will likely be temporary if at all. Change in your outer world will only occur as a result of change in your inner world.

Prior to making any judgment in regard to your success or lack of success with the **Law of Attraction** and attaining your ideal health, you must instinctively understand that all Power comes from within (review chapters 1 and 2 if necessary).

Control Your Thoughts

Imagine that if you think it, believe it, and expect it, it will materialize. Therefore, a destructive thought is your personal devil. It can ruin your progress to your ideal health. Controlling your thoughts and ensuring that they are constructive and empowering is the way you tap into the Unlimited Power within you.

Much health related challenges today are a result of

obesity. Therefore, we have chosen weight loss as an example and will guide you through each step to show you how you apply the teachings in this book to improve your health.

> *"This topic is one that is near and dear to me because I have been plump to heavy most of my adult life until about four years ago. I am now 80 lbs lighter than the heaviest time of my life. I once was a size 16, and of course even larger right after the pregnancy of my son. I am now a size 6 (sometimes an 8 depending on the cut). I know this works, but you have to expect it to work and begin to live the life as if you were already there, then the Universe will deliver what you need to get there."* ~Tammy Lynch

Is there a difference between hoping to lose weight and knowing you will? Certainly there is. There's also a difference between trying to lose weight and really truly deciding to do so. When you really decide that you will accomplish your weight loss goal and you know that nothing will prevent you from achieving it, when you truly know that you have the will and the Power within, and you expect it as sure as the sun rising in the morning, then you are guaranteed to attain your goal.

If you say, "*I'll try to lose weight*" or "*I'll give it a shot*" then you likely will <u>not</u> lose the weight you desire, because the undertone and true belief is that it's difficult for you and won't likely happen. Even this subtle undertone is destructive thought, and you have to eliminate these thoughts as much as possible. You must have the faith that your desired result is certain or you *"will"* achieve what you know to be certain. You must absolutely know that you will attain it. Success is guaranteed. For when you know it to be true then, and only then, it will it become true for you.

Once you know that success is guaranteed, you begin to plan accordingly. As it relates to weight loss, your planning will likely include diet and exercise. It may also include a visit to your doctor. If you don't start doing this type of planning, then you don't expect to lose weight "do you?" Ultimately, when you expect to be successful, you act differently than when you don't expect success. Begin to act with successful expectations.

During this process, it is essential that you protect your mind from negative, destructive thoughts and focus upon positive, successful, empowering thoughts. When a destructive, disempowering thought enters your mind, it is imperative that you go through the process immediately of eliminating that destructive thought (review chapters 3 and 4 if necessary).

Vision Statements

Making Vision Statements a daily part of your life is necessary in order to attract what you desire. When you pray, add the appropriate *Vision Statements* to your daily prayers. Prayers are most successful when they claim what you desire, and are spoken in the form of intentions, versus the more common practice of prayer, which is hoping and wishing. Yes, we are confirming everything you've been told about prayers...they are much more powerful when they have the element of faith. Similarly, so do these *Vision Statements*.

The Vision Statements below give you a great selection to get started.

We recommend that you add your own to the mix as well. Choose the statements that best assist you with your health situation, and write them down. Note them in your handheld; write them in your journal, and anywhere else you can have access to them twenty-four hours a day.

Health

- My body is perfect, strong, powerful, loving and harmonious.
- My body is meant to be perfectly healthy.
- My body and the cells within my body respond to my positive thoughts and it keeps me healthy.

- I love my body.
- I have been fortunate to have the physical body that I have, which has served me well.
- With each breath I take, healing energy is flowing through my body, keeping me in perfect health.
- I am happy and healthy.
- My body always cures it self.
- I am vibrant, healthy and active, and it feels great.
- I am so grateful for my perfect health and true wealth.
- Today is going to settle any stressful issue. I will feel at peace at the end of the day.
- I am at home in my body
- My body has been a good friend to me.

Weight Loss

- My body is perfect, strong, powerful, loving and harmonious.
- I feed my body through good foods and beverages, and give it the exercise it needs.
- My body's present appearance is a result of the past. Today I am an active, healthy person, and my body is responding.
- I get more attractive every day.
- The intelligent cells throughout my body know how to achieve my ideal body weight and they are working toward that right now.

- I love my body.
- Exercise is fun.
- I'm very fortunate to have a high metabolism.
- My body, muscles, bones and all my vital organs enjoy the results of my activity, which makes exercise enjoyable.
- I love being at my ideal body weight.
- The energy flowing through my body delivers life to all the cells and this life flow of energy keeps me feeling healthy and young.
- I'm getting younger and healthier every day.
- I look younger and younger every day.
- My muscles are firm and tone.
- My body produces the necessary regeneration of cells to keep my skin smooth and young looking.
- Being my ideal body weight feels so good, that I don't ever want to lose that feeling.
- My appetite only tells me I'm hungry when my body needs nourishment.
- I have more energy than most people I know.
- I feel alive and full of energy.

It is vital to your success to repeatedly say the *Vision Statements*. We suggest that you read your *Vision Statements* no less than four times per day.

For weight loss, you should begin and end your day and each meal with your *Vision Statements*. Other times when your *Vision Statements* come in handy is when you feel hungry, don't want to exercise, want a snack that's not good for you, have destructive thoughts, and before social events involving food and alcohol.

As you begin making these statements, you might say to yourself, *"that's not what my body is really like"* or *"this isn't really true."* You must get those thoughts out of your mind immediately. You are to dream in perfect idealism.

Let's use an example... if you say *"I love my body"* and deep down you think, *"not really,"* then you must find a way to eliminate the *"not really"* thought.

1. Become a *Master* at eliminating disempowering thoughts at will. This is a learned behavior and can be mastered, but only through practice. Meditation (chapter 8) often helps in mastering the elimination of thought.

2. Substitute the destructive thought with one that is more empowering. When the thought *"not really"* enters your mind, challenge that thought by saying something similar to the following:

> *"Maybe I don't feel like I love my body right now, but in reality, I'm alive and it's been there for me. It has served me well in many memorable times. I have enjoyed so much with my family and I'm able to work full time because my body*

> has been there for me. Really my body is awesome; I'm thankful for my body and what I've been able to accomplish with it."

> "Right now, my body is simply a result of my past thoughts, so it's not my body that's the problem, it's my past thoughts. My current thoughts are going to give the cells in my body what it needs to attain my ideal health and weight."

Any disempowering thought can be substituted logically with better thoughts. You are perfect, strong, powerful, loving and harmonious. It is your natural state, and any other state has been brought on by negative or disempowering thoughts and beliefs. Get in the habit of spinning your thoughts to your benefit, not your detriment.

3. Re-write the *Vision Statement* to one that is more believable. Here are a couple examples:

> "I love the fact that my body is improving the way it looks day by day."

> "The love I feel about my body is improving every day."

> "I will love my body even more when I attain my ideal weight."

Controlling your thoughts to focus upon those that support what you do desire is essential to manifesting your desires. It is <u>The Secret!!</u> Only your thoughts and imagination will create the vision that can be delivered to you in the outer world.

Create-a-Vision

Your imagination is extremely powerful and is the primary process that you will use to design the new healthy you. Whatever picture you can vividly imagine in your minds eye, can become your reality. Can you dream, imagine, and create without limitation? If you can, you can attract it into your life.

In your mind's eye, create the perfect, healthy, ideal you. See how slim you are. Feel how great it feels to be your ideal weight. See yourself exercising and enjoying it. See, hear and feel what it's like to get compliments from others on how great you look.

You can spark your creativity by gathering photos of figures that would represent your ideal weight. Go through fashion magazines and gather photos of the clothing you intend to buy once you achieve your ideal weight.

An awesome visualization tool is to take a photo of someone with the physical body that resembles the body you are trying to create, and place it on your vehicle's dashboard face up. Ideally, the body in the photo is physically proportionate to what you desire to become. On the photo, write this sentence, "*This is the dress that fits me perfectly*", or whatever is appropriate. The sun, even when the skies are gray, reflects the photo onto the windshield and you get to look at that reflection everywhere you drive. It's pretty awesome. It doesn't matter that the words are a mirror image, or that the photo was cut out of a magazine, your subconscious knows what the words say, and it doesn't know the difference between fiction and reality, so you will begin the process of reprogramming your subconscious mind in regards to the body you have.

For some, creating a vision of idealism could be the most difficult of the processes we suggest, but nevertheless, is the most essential. Meditation not only will assist in giving you the clarity of thinking you'll need, but is the method in which concentrated thought becomes powerful.

The trick to all of this and any **Law of Attraction** goal is to begin living like you have already accomplished the goal. What does a person of your desired weight eat daily? What do they do for exercise? What other habits do they have? Start acting the part. Become in consciousness the weight you desire. Once you have accepted yourself as the person you are becoming, then you will get what you need in your outer world to achieve it.

Allow for the Best Outcome

There is only one moment and it is this moment that you must focus upon. Control your thoughts to focus upon the most productive thing you must do right now. Don't worry about how long it will take to achieve your goal. Don't focus upon how difficult it will be. Simply act in this moment as if success is guaranteed.

Procrastination will get you nowhere. Once you decide, you must act then be consciously open to the possibilities around you.

Any new product, service, or invention is first imagined in the mind of its creator. Any great athlete or performer imagines their perfect performance prior to it coming to fruition. Any great architect imagines the structure in which they intend to build prior to putting it to paper in final form. In all of these cases, the picture of the desired end result must first be vivid in thought before it ever can materialize in reality.

Today it is necessary to dream perfect dreams. Don't worry about the current reality. Imagine a beautiful or handsome, slender, healthy, peaceful you and the Universe will correspond to your command. Life will be rearranged and become for you, and to you, that which you have imagined.

Visualize the perfect image, and hold it in you mind.

Feel the way it feels. The rest will unfold and you will be lead to your desires. You will be given opportunities that will expand and develop into that which you desire. You will be inspired to take a path at precisely the right time that will result in the right effect.

Today, begin to expect that you will attain your desired weight. Don't question the process just begin to act upon your vision.

- *Choose your vision statements and begin repeating them*
- *Meditate and dream your perfect dream daily*
- *Talk with your doctor to ensure you get off to a healthy start*
- *Research and plan your diet. Plan every meal and begin eating as if you were at your ideal weight*
- *Identify your exercise routine*
- *Only weight yourself once per week, at the same time and with the same amount of clothing on.*
- *Start shopping in the magazines and online for the photos that will remind you of how you will look and feel once you have attained your ideal weight.*
- *Start making decisions right now from a point of consciousness that has already attained your ideal weight.*
- *Act as if you are already there!!*

Most importantly, continue to dream perfect dreams and keep disempowering thoughts out of your mind at this very moment and every moment hereafter. Allow the *Unlimited Power of the Infinite* to guide you to the new you.

MY THOUGHTS:

CHAPTER 10

"Manifesting Abundant Wealth"

Your financial wealth today is a result of your past beliefs, which were created by your thoughts and feelings. Your behavior of the recent past is a reflection of your beliefs, which are a result of your past thoughts and feelings. Ultimately your past thoughts and feelings created the chain of events that resulted in your current financial wealth or lack thereof.

Whether it's health, wealth or love, it's the same story. However, just as any other aspect of your life, you can decide to improve your current financial condition. The moment that you put aside your beliefs regarding the lack of financial prosperity in your life is the moment in which you will begin to attract financial prosperity into your life. The moment that you know that success is guaranteed, and that you now are living the life of someone who is worthy of financial success, is the moment in which the Universe will begin to set the forces in motion to deliver it to you.

How do people who are worthy of financial success act? What do they think about that is different than what you have done in your recent past? To become in consciousness that which you desire to be, you must begin to act as if you are already that person.

So you will need to make some changes in the way you think and your everyday behavior, one moment at a time.

The changes will include how you think about spending, saving and investing among other things. The changes will also include the thoughts about your future. How you enjoy your prosperity. How you help others as a result of fortune. These improved thoughts about money will change your beliefs and ultimately will result in an improved financial condition.

Ask yourself *"what does someone who's wealthy do differently than I?"* If you truly know you'll attain your financial freedom, then you must begin to think, feel and act as someone with financial freedom. This doesn't mean that you spend money you don't have like someone who has it. That would not be financially responsible, would it? This means you begin to think about your next investment, your next vacation, and your next material gift to yourself and others.

When the topic of money comes up, you don't discuss how you don't have enough, in fact most truly wealthy people don't discuss how much or how little money they have because it isn't an issue. They don't typically share how they plan on investing; saving or spending their money as if it should be public knowledge either. Internal focus and reflection is crucial and the key.

As long as you believe you will achieve financial freedom then subconsciously you will begin acting as one that already has financial freedom. In the alternative, if you have difficulty believing you will achieve financial freedom then begin acting as you already have it, and you will create the faith needed.

To get started, you must first decide to change your behavior. The mind and body cannot be separate. For example, if you behave like you already make wise financial decisions, your subconscious will quickly believe that you make wise financial decisions, and you therefore will begin attracting wise financial opportunities.

Do you think that those with financial freedom choose to spend every last dollar they have on something that will not give them a return? Do you think they think about the things they cannot afford? Of course not! Those that are truly fortunate don't talk about money much at all, and when they do, it certainly isn't about the lack of money. What they do is plan how they are going to invest, spend and contribute.

So as with all aspects of the **Law of Attraction**, you must first become wealthy in consciousness. It is essential that you first make decisions about money wisely, just like someone with who's financially successful.

Let's go through the steps just as we did with "Creating Abundant Health"...

- All Power Comes from Within
- Control Your Thoughts
- Vision Statements
- Create-a-Vision
- Allow for the Best Outcome

All Power Comes From Within

You can no longer blame, or credit something other than yourself for your current financial situation.

We recognize that you may have been born in a family that has never had financial freedom, or you may have had a situation arise that drained your finances. However, it is within your control to change it. It is essential to recognize this to be true. If you don't believe this is true, then consciously or subconsciously, you may continue to blame some circumstance that you believe is outside of your control for where you're at today and this ultimately, will keep you right where you are today.

Your expectations in life, whether desired or not, are shaped by your beliefs, and your beliefs are a product of your conscious thought. If the Infinite is within you, then His power is within you. Do you believe that God has the Power to deliver you financial freedom? Do you think that the Divine has the resources to find a way to guide you to financial freedom? Do you think that any of us were meant to live in poverty?

You cannot be to others the best you can be unless you are secure and happy with whom you are. Since the Universe is abundant in all things, why does it make sense for you not to be abundantly wealthy? With financial wealth, you have no worries and can therefore be more to everyone else in the Universe.

The Infinite creates through the individual. Therefore if the *Infinite* has the power and resources to guide you to financial wealth, and He creates through the individual, then it is you that has the power.

However, none of this works if you don't believe you have this *Power*. You do have the *Power*. It lies within you. It is the "I" within you that is united with the *Infinite* resources of your *Higher Power*, which will ensure your successful result, if you believe.

If you instinctively understand that all power comes from within, then the seed that will grow into financial success has already been planted (review chapters 1 and 2, if necessary).

Control Your Thoughts

The thoughts of fear that come with the lack of money can ruin your progress to financial freedom.

Controlling your thoughts and ensuring that they are constructive and empowering is essential to your success.

Fear, which results when you focus upon the lack of money, is the most negative emotion that you can have and definitely is not in vibrational alignment with the *All-Powerful* Universe.

Remember that fear is never a thought that will allow you to attract anything through the Infinite. It's just a thought that stays with you and eats away at your self-confidence. It kills your enthusiasm, promotes procrastination, and stifles your creativity.

Fear is the most useless emotion and should be taken as a sign to change your thoughts immediately. The only use for a fearful thought is that it makes you realize that your thinking is not where it should be. If you continue thinking fearfully you will be pushing those things you desire further away.

You must have the faith that financial freedom is a birthright. Part of that process is to ensure that you begin thinking and acting like someone who has financial freedom.

Once you know that success is guaranteed, you begin to plan and act accordingly. As it relates to wealth, here are some habits that wealthy people live by.

- Define your goals.
- Aim above those that are considered mediocre.
- Obtain the education your lacking. This may not necessarily be formal education, it could be as simple as reading a couple books.
- Set systems in place to ensure you do the important things first. Then be disciplined to to do them.
- Don't procrastinate. The time will never be better for you to do what you don't like to do. You must do those things first.
- Finish what you start. If you make a commitment, follow it through. Make follow through and reliability a habit.
- Control your urges and desires and ensure that what you spend your time and money on give you a return.
- Eliminate the "glass half empty" philosophy and always find the best in everything.
- Be creative!!

As always, it is essential that you protect your mind from negative, destructive thoughts and focus upon positive, successful, empowering thoughts. When a destructive, disempowering thought enters your mind, it is imperative that you go through the process immediately of eliminating that destructive thought (review chapters 3 and 4 if necessary).

Vision Statements

As we did with our health, we will do with wealth as well. Choose the statements that you're most comfortable with and add a few of your own.

Financial Wealth

- I'm so thankful for finding the path that is continuing to lead me to financial freedom.
- I make excellent money decisions.
- Wealth is drawn to me.
- I am open and receptive to new avenues of income.
- I recognize inspired thought as an opportunity to expand and improve my income.
- I attract money and opportunity
- I am worthy of financial wealth.
- I am a money magnet.
- My current financial situation is only a result of the past. Today I have ascended to a new level. Today I am a millionaire, and it's just a matter of time when the Universe will show the world and me this truth.
- I allow my income to expand, as I am worthy of financial freedom and wealth.
- All the money I spend helps others and results in an investment in my future that is returned to me in greater abundance.
- I have multiple streams of income that support my desired lifestyle.

- I am financially free.
- My part time work is investing my money and creating multiple streams of passive income.
- I visualize in my mind's eye the financial success that's my birthright. It is this vision that fills my life with abundance.
- I use the Power of Intention to create wealth and abundance – My intention is inevitable.
- I replicate the success principles of wealthy and successful people by incorporating them into my life.
- Money provides the flexibility and freedom that makes life more enjoyable.
- Money flows to me in avalanches of abundance.
- Unexpected income is attracted to me often from a variety of sources on a continual basis.
- I am worthy of wealth and abundance
- I am becoming wealthier, happier, and more free ever day.
- I deserve wealth and abundance.
- I manage my time, thoughts and money wisely.
- All of the money that I gift comes back to me multiplied.
- I am open to receiving, and I am a generous giver, each is important in the cycle of financial well-being.
- Awesome and exciting opportunities for prosperity constantly come my way.
- My capacity to earn money, and to generate additional income, increases with each and every day.

Career Advancement

- I choose to work because I enjoy my work.
- I always work with and for wonderful people.
- I love my work.
- I am capable and organized.
- I am extremely efficient and get more done in less time than most.
- I am a decisive and productive decision maker.
- I follow through with tasks and take responsibility.
- I never blame others for my accomplishments. I know that it is me that makes the difference.
- Success is guaranteed and a birthright.
- Life and work is simple and pleasurable.
- Whatever my inner voice tells me to do, will be a success.
- Whatever my employer guides me to do, will be a success and rewarding.
- I love my work and it is the satisfaction of doing a job well that feels good. If I passionately execute, the money automatically follows.
- All areas of my life and work are abundant and over flowing.
- I am grateful for the success I've experienced.
- Everything I touch becomes successful.
- I enjoy my work and it has financially served me well.
- I always work with and for wonderful people.
- I am grateful for the success I've experienced.

Repeat your selected Vision Statements a minimum

of four times per day and any time something occurs that sparks the thought of fear, or the lack of enough money.

If you mentally resist one of the statements, and starting thinking how *"untrue"* it is, then you must immediately get those thoughts out of your head. Your picture must be perfect. Your current reality has nothing to do with your future.

Let's use an example... if you say *"Money flows to me in avalanches of abundance."* and after you repeat this you say to yourself, *"yeah, right,"* then you must find a way to eliminate the *"yeah, right"* thought. It could be as simply as saying, "Yeah right is right. It may not have happened in the past, but I'm changing that right NOW!"

Below is a reminder of some of the steps you can take to help in eliminating this destructive thinking.

1. *Become a master at eliminating disempowering thoughts at will.*

2. *Substitute the destructive thought with one that is more empowering.*

3. *Re-write the Vision Statement to one that is more believable.*

Create-a-Vision

Be creative and remember there are no limitations. The picture you can vividly imagine can become your reality.

In your mind's eye, create the vision of your perfect home, the car you want to drive, the clothes you want to own, the social environments you want to enjoy. See yourself at a charity auction and you donating significantly to your favorite the cause. Feel how it feels to be able to contribute to needy causes. See yourself enjoying a dinner party in your new home. Create a vision of you in your new job.

1. Determine exactly how much money you desire and write it down.
2. Identify the date in which you intend to attain the money and write it down.
3. Write down the vision statements that include the amount of money you desire and the time in which you intend to attain it.
4. Create-a-Vision of the scenario in which you are enjoying the money that you attained and a vision of holding the actual amount you desire.
5. Repeat your Vision Statements at least twice daily (four or more times is better) and meditate daily for at least 15 minutes focusing upon the Create-a-Visions with all of the feeling you'd have if you had

already achieved your vision.

It is important that you do all of these steps. Become in consciousness that which you desire. Once you have accepted yourself as the wealthy person you are becoming, only then will you begin to achieve it.

Allow for the Best Outcome

When opportunity knocks, you have to open the door. This is not a time for indecision or doubt, over caution or worry.

Inspired thoughts, unique opportunities, gut feelings, and intuition are all ways in which solutions will be presented to you. When these come your way, you must act.

Most importantly, continue to dream in perfect idealism and keep disempowering thoughts out of your head one moment at a time. Be perceptive and the *Infinite* with its unlimited resources will guide you.

MY THOUGHTS:

CHAPTER 11

"Attracting Abundant Love"

The *"Mastery of Abundant Living"* can only truly be mastered if you are living all the Laws of attraction. At the heart of the **Law of Attraction** is that very thing that is at the heart of all human beings which is the one emotion, feeling, driving desire, most talked about, most sung about, most anything'd about thing which is that four letter word called "*love*". You only have to turn on the radio to any music station and within minutes a song will be played whose principle message is that of *love*. The movie industry has no end of titles to movies and many hundreds more whose basic theme is circled around something to do with love.

We sing about it, we write about it, we talk about it, and we spend most of our life seeking more of it in one way or another. Yet it is one of the most misunderstood and illusive things in the lives of literally hundreds of millions of people throughout the world. How can something that brings so much light into our lives be something that eludes so many?

All Power Comes from Within

To be able to capitalize on the full nature of the **Law of Attraction**, it is essential that you become loving to others. You attract that which you become in consciousness. In order to be able to receive love you must love yourself. Like attracts like, birds of a feather flock together, give and receive, do unto others as you would have them do unto you, and the list of sayings and quotations goes on and on that leads us to an understanding that what we send out will be returned to us in some form or another.

If you feel hate, it will stay with you until you're able to release it. If you feel love, because it's in alignment with the *Infinite*, you will attract love in multiplied proportions. That should be simple to understand and simple to apply. But for many, many people, it is something they have yet to *Master*.

The *Natural Law* of the Universe is simple and when applied in its simple form always returns to you the same *but multiplied*. Respect, love, light, truth and peace; is there anything more virtuous then this? To experience this you must be aligned with the principles, which guide them.

In order to give love, you must first possess love for yourself. Can you respect others if you don't first have respect for yourself? Can you give truth if you are not first truthful with yourself? Can you love others if you do not first love yourself? Of course the answer to all these questions is a resounding "no".

What if your barrier to loving others is that of first loving yourself?

There is a very simply way to change your attitude toward yourself and while it is simple; it is not always simple for everyone to do. You probably have seen many times in a love scene in a movie or had occasion where you yourself or a close friend was faced with that moment in time where they looked in the eyes of that person they had deep affection for and the words which express that very affection to the other were to be spoken. You have heard these three words in songs, in books and across the big screen dozens' if not hundreds of times. But how many times have you spoken these words to yourself?

The first place to start in showing more love to others around you and the world is by first opening the one door that is the most important of all doors to open. That door where you reside and from where all that flows from you comes. The "I" in the "I am." When you can look yourself in the eye and say those three words that so many people look to hear spoken to them, these three words will set you free from the bonds of negative emotions and feelings that bring about so much ill in your life, the world and the Universe. In order to love one another, we all must first be able to love our self.

You might find this easy or you might find this hard, but no matter whether hard or easy, you need to do this one thing. Do this everyday for as long as it takes until you can feel it inside. Many people find themselves in tears when they do this.

Go to a quiet place where you can be alone, which is usually the bathroom. You need a mirror to do this so the bathroom not only gives you a quiet place but provides a mirror as well. With no one else around and in the quiet solitude of that place you have decided on, look into the mirror at your reflection. First look around at your face noticing your hair, your ears, your mouth, your nose and then your eyes. When you get to your eyes, continue to focus directly on looking into them going back and forth from one eye to another. You will start to realize that you are looking directly through the window of your eyes into your soul. You will start to feel that you are looking at the "I" within you, your spiritual connection to the *Infinite*. At the moment that you begin to realize that you are looking at the personage inside the body, that is the time to utter the words which will tell you how you feel about yourself. Say the words, "*I love you.*"

Continue to look into your eyes when you say the words. Give yourself a few seconds, and then say the words again. Say them in a way that you know the truthfulness of the words. If you begin crying, enjoy the experience. Cherish this moment in your life where you are now and release any bad feelings you have about yourself. If need be, forgive yourself for anything you feel in this moment that you need to forgive yourself for. Tell the "I" in you that from this day forward you are going to do, say and be everything you need to be. At last, say the words, "*I am in love with you.*"

When you love yourself and most importantly, when you can be "*in love*" with yourself, you can love others and you can be "*in love*" with that special someone in your life or will be led to that special someone that you can be "*in love*" with. You can now live the *Natural Laws* of the Universe and in harmony with respect, love, light, truth and peace because you have now allowed your self to apply these principles in your life to the "I" in the "I am." The more you make loving yourself one of the predominant thoughts in your mind and the more love you will give to others around you, the more love, abundance and prosperity will be manifested in all areas of your life.

Now remember that feeling and your conversation with yourself, and this is your new Create-a-Vision for Love. The perfect picture of loving yourself you can easily duplicate in your minds eye.

Control Your Thoughts

In order to receive the abundant love that the Universe has ready at your doorstep to give to you, you must first release any feelings that you harbor that are in direct opposition to the law. If you have feelings of resentment, hate, jealousy, or envy just to name a few, you cannot feel or experience the full impact and nature of the **Law of Love**. Remember light and darkness cannot occupy the same space. Positive and negative thoughts cannot co-exist. If you harbor negative feelings for anyone or anything, you create a barrier to the one thing people all over the world desire the most. To receive love, you must first love and in order to give love, you must first love yourself.

Think about how you are feeling right now. Your feelings tell you if you are on the right course or headed in a direction that is not consistent with what you desire. How do you feel about those that are close to you right now? Does a smile come to your face, or is there a pit in your stomach that won't go away? Do you have good feelings or bad feelings about someone or something? Holding on to feelings that make us feel bad is what makes you feel even worse. It also makes those in you like feel bad. More so, it even creates dis-ease. Dis-ease is what creates disease.

Have you ever noticed that the people around you that are sick the most are often the people who have the most negative feelings about themselves and others. Have you noticed that the people who seldom get ill are the most positive people you know?

So... eliminate the disempowering thoughts about others and substitute the negative thoughts with positive thoughts. Look for the best in everyone. Find something you respect or like in everyone and focus upon those things in him or her.

The very minute, the very second that you change your thoughts and begin living the **Law of Love** and the natural laws of respect, light, truth and peace, your life will take a 180 degree turn and you will begin to experience greater love, prosperity and abundance in your life. *It is a law!* When you act within the law, you become subject to it. You will reap the benefits of the law just as certain as you reap the harsh reality of its retribution when you are not acting in accordance with it.

As soon as you change from negative and destructive thoughts of envy, hate, despair, jealousy and all other negative emotions that bar you from receiving your true desires to those feelings that encircle the **Law of Love**, you will immediate begin feeling the realities and manifestations that come with those feelings. You will feel it in your very heart. Release the negative and embrace the positive and your body will immediately tell you via your feelings that you are now in the right place. All that you attract to you from that point on will be in harmony with the **Law of Love**.

Vision Statements

As we did with health and wealth, we will do with love as well. Choose the statements that you're most comfortable with and add a few of your own. Repeat them daily at least two times per day, or whenever you're feeling disempowering thought of another.

Releasing Negative Feelings

- Resentment does not benefit anyone or me and is an artificial feeling. It is only I that can control my thoughts and feelings.
- I won't allow anyone else to influence my day negatively.
- I have a shield around me that protects me from the impact of negative words of others.
- I forgive others, because I have the power to create my life the way I want it to be, and no one else.
- My heart loves all the time. Not only do I forgive, I let go and release all negative feelings of others.
- Criticism can't hurt me, as what others think are not important in relation to what I think.
- The past will no longer affect my future, as forgiveness and love for others and myself is what allows today to be joyous.
- I happily release all that I no longer need, and all that no longer serves me well.
- Thank you for my freedom from old past hurts.
- Forgiving others makes me feel free, in control, and one with God and everyone and everything in the Universe.
- Destructive thoughts and beliefs I release. I have

no doubts and no fears, as I am one with God and God takes care of his children and gives me eternal life.
- Blame, worry, and guilt are useless emotions because I have the power to change any situation that I'm not happy with.
- If He is willing to forgive me, than I owe it to Him to forgive myself.
- It is not my place to judge, as it is the differences among us that create the synergy of growth, and without the differences, we'd be a dying Universe.
- I accept people for whom they are and contribute to the well being of the Universe by remaining positive, and showing love to all I encounter.

Feelings and Love

- I love life. I look forward to every second of every day.
- Everything I do brings me happiness and joy.
- My life is getting better and better with each passing day.
- Happiness is abundant in my life.
- It feels great to smile and show appreciation and love to others.
- Smiling makes me and everyone I encounter happier.
- I feel better when I smile, and that's why I smile all the time.
- I decide each day how I'm going to feel, and I

have decided to feel good everyday, for the rest of my life.
- I am united with God, and therefore, have His Infinite ability to create good in my life.
- I am meant for greatness. I am special and my unique individualism brings only what I can bring to this Universe.
- Life is like a joyous party, where everyone and everything is having a blast.
- The more I love myself the more others love me and the more happiness I feel within.
- I respect and love everyone, as I know that the more I love others, the more I will be loved.
- Love is the Universal Law that drives everything. I continue to find reasons to be more loving every day.

Peace and Harmony

- The more love I give, the more love I get.
- The more harmonious I am, the more my life has harmony.
- The more peaceful I am, the more peace I experience.
- The more joyous I am, the more my life is joyous.
- I'm so happy and blessed that everything goes my way.
- People love me.
- Everything goes right for me.
- Today there will be no conflicts and I will be in perfect harmony with the Holy Spirit within me and within everyone and everything in the

Universe.
- Differences will be soothed even before they arise, as I will feel the love among every one I touch, and where there's love, there's understanding.
- There is love in all of my relationships, even casual friendships.
- I am Love.
- Love is a constant energy within me, and everyone who meets or knows me can feel the love I have for them.
- Others see me as a loving compassionate person.
- Every day I feel more and more love from others and for others.
- I love myself.
- I love my life.
- People love me.
- I have love for everyone and everything in the Universe.
- Everyone can feel the love that I radiate.
- Only positive, constructive, loving words do I say to others and myself.
- Love surrounds and takes care of me.
- I have an abundant amount of loving people who fill my life and it is easy to show them love.
- I am my best friend and the words that I say to myself are filled with love and compassion.

<u>Create-a-Vision</u>

In your mind's eye, create the vision of the perfect loving relationships, that perfect companion, kind and loving friendships, the social groups you want to enjoy. Be creative and remember there are no limitations. The picture you can vividly imagine can become your reality. See yourself holding hands with that special someone; enjoying friendly conversation, everyone is smiling. Feel how it feels to have such loving friends surrounding you and that special significant other that loves you. Create a vision of you with these new loving relationships.

1. Determine exactly what kind of relationship you desire

2. Write down the vision statements that include the kinds of relationships you desire.

3. Create a Vision of the scenario in which you are enjoying the perfect relationship and a vision of being in that relationship.

4. Repeat your Vision Statements at least twice daily (four times is better) and meditate daily for at least 15 minutes focusing upon the Create-a-Visions with all of the feeling you'd have if you had already achieved your vision.

It is important that you do all of these steps. Become in consciousness that which you desire. Once you have accepted yourself as the loving person you are becoming, and you accept yourself as someone who only sees the good in others, only then will you begin to attract the love in your life that you have only dreamed of.

Allow for the Best Outcome

As will all "allowing" you have to be open to what is being presented. As long as you focus on how you want to feel and leave the picture of who will make you feel this way open for possibilities, then success is guaranteed. So many place figures and faces to their loving relationships that when someone who is perfect for you arrives into your life, you don't recognize it.

When opportunity comes, you have to open the door. This is not a time for indecision or doubt, over caution or worry. Focus on how you want to feel and don't be afraid to enter into a relationship openly and lovingly, staying detached from the outcome and allowing the *Universe* to direct while the relationship that you were meant to have unfolds before you.

MY THOUGHTS:

CHAPTER 12

Quantum Physics Basics

We are co-creators with our Universe. Our thoughts are linked to invisible energy and they determine what the energy forms. Your thoughts literally shift the universe on a particle-by-particle basis to create your physical life. Everything around you in physical form started with an idea, the idea grew as it was shared and expressed, until alas it became manifested into its physical form, which you can now touch, taste, and smell, hear and/or see. The world around us literally becomes what we think about most.

The world is not the hard and unchangeable thing it may appear to be and this is proven by Quantum physics. It is a very fluid place continuously built up using our individual and collective states of thought. Even our very bodies are an ocean of continuously moving matter.

Nobel prize winning physicists have proven beyond doubt that the physical world is one large sea of energy that flashes into and out of being billions of times a second, over and over again. In the world of Quantum Physics they have shown that thoughts are what puts together and holds together this ever-changing energy field into the "objects" that we see. Let's break down what makes up the human body. The plasmatic matter that is in the Universe is the basis of all that is and thoughts are the mold that moves this matter into form.

What is the human body made of? The body is comprised of tissues and organs, which are made of cells. These cells make up the bones, organs, muscles, and circulatory system, which move blood through the body supplying it with the needed nutrients to fuel all the cells. What are cells made of? Molecules. The Molecules are made of Atoms, which are made from sub-atomic particles. And finally science has discovered that these sub-atomic particles are made of electrons, which is a form of *Energy*.

All things originate in thought and appear physically as a result of thought directing electrons or energy. It is thought that gives all matter form in our physical world. For every effect there is a cause. If we follow the trail of every effect backward in time we will find the creative thought from which it grew.

This is absolutely mind-boggling. The electrons of a ball are not in the shape of a ball unless we believe it's a ball. This is how we manifest our thoughts and beliefs into our reality. We simply believe it and electrons shape it to be so.

Your physical body, among other things, is a huge collective of constantly changing *Energy* and you control it all with your powerful *Mind*. You are one big stellar and powerful *Human Being*, which is controlled and formed by your very thoughts.

The mind that controls the cells of your body is one with our subconscious mind. Cells are intelligent and act without thought or conscious knowledge. They are responsive to the *"will"* of our conscious mind. This is the explanation for metaphysical healing. The power of a belief in the subconscious mind also provides for manifestations as it relates to our bodies.

A person's *very powerful* thoughts can heal organs, repair broken and damaged tissues and much more, many times to the amazement of science and others all which are most referred to as miraculous.

Man is a spiritual being but he also has a material or physical body. Everything in the physical realm is relative while those things in the Spiritual realm are absolute. The relative physical realm is always shaping itself to the absolute forces of the *Spiritual World*. And that force is the very thought process that all humans possess. Without thought, there would be no physical manifestation. It is with those very powerful thoughts that some are able to focus upon so well that causes a physical manifestation of healing. We often refer to this as miracles.

While most people are not aware of it, on a daily basis second by second, minute-by-minute, hour upon hour, everyone is causing things to manifest into their lives based on the thoughts they have. Quantum physics looks into the realm of the very matter and elements of what those thoughts are working upon. As people become aware of the fact that their thoughts are what molds their universe, they can empower themselves to affect their reality in a positive way.

Ignorance is not bliss. To be ignorant of what is causing ones reality is to continue to allow your thoughts to continue to give you the same results in your life. The reality you experience on a daily basis is the effect of the thoughts, which you have. When you change the cause you get a different affect. Thus, whether you think you can or think you can't, you are right either way. What you think you can accomplish, you can. What you think you cannot accomplish, you can't.

This is the reason that ninety-five percent of people live in a world of lack and need. They are focused upon effect and trying to fix life based on what they observe. Rather then taking the things that they observe and understanding the cause and working to change their very thoughts, which will create a different effect.

By understanding the **Law of Attraction** and that it is working at all times in your life and by having a basic understanding of Quantum physics and that your thoughts are the mold upon which the plasmatic material of the Universe is molded, you can begin to change your outer world from your world within.

To continue to live life with the belief that everything in your life is out of your control and to blame others for your circumstances is to live a life of denial. By accepting the reality of what is occurring in our life as being that of your own, you can begin to change the very world you live in. You can change the world in your immediate area, the world as a whole and the Universe that surrounds you.

How fast can you change the world around you?

To understand the **Law of Attraction** as it relates to Quantum physics you simply have to understand how fast your thoughts are manifested in the Universe.

Light travels about 186,000 miles a second and electrons are pure negative electricity and have the same potential speed as all other cosmic energy such as light, electricity and thought. In essence, electrons travel similarly to the speed of light, which is almost instantaneous when it's within our human sight.

Fortunately, the things that come into your life right now do not manifest at the speed of thought, not quite yet anyhow. This can be a good thing. Until you have mastered your thoughts, you really don't want things manifesting in your life at the speed of thought. However, as you *Master* your thoughts, and begin to manifest things that you really desire with perfect precision, then you will begin to accelerate the process. Use your thoughts wisely. Don't waste time on negative thinking. The negative thoughts of today will be down time in the future.

So keep perfect positive thoughts aligned with what you truly desire and the Universe will move the plasmatic matter that is there to correspond with that which you desire. The minute you have the empowering thought that is heart centered and believed with true conviction, the Universe is moving to correspond with it and manifest what you desire. The more you nurture the thought, the sooner it will become manifest to you.

Understanding how Quantum physics relates to the **Law of Attraction** can be explained very simply and you don't have to be a Quantum Physicist to appreciate it. Everyone understands what the speed-of-light is. If you were to physically travel from the Earth to the nearest galaxy it would take you 3,000,000 light-years to get there. However, when you have a thought, it is *immediately* there.

Our thoughts span the Universe. Every person who believes in God has to believe this. Every time you say a prayer you believe with all your heart that God is hearing you. This means that you believe that your very thoughts are spanning the Universe to get to Him.

Understanding that our thoughts span the Universe helps us to understand that the minute we have a thought, whether it is negative or positive, our immediate universe around us is changed. When you change your thoughts to those that work in harmony with Universal principles and laws, you immediately change the world around you and the things that will become manifest in your life will be in direct alignment with them.

To live in *"Harmonic Abundance"*, you must think thoughts that are in harmony with the Universe.

MY THOUGHTS:

CHAPTER 13

Vision Statements for Life

Vision statements are essential to creating a new belief. They plant the seed that germinates and flourishes into an empowering new belief. Many vision statements for health, wealth and love are noted in chapters 10 – 12. Below are some additional vision statements that you can use to help you manifest your desires.

Abundance

- Life was meant to be abundant. The Universe has enough prosperity in all aspects for everyone and everything.
- All areas of my life are full of abundance.
- All of the good and abundance in the world is at my command.
- The Universe has Infinite resources; there is plenty enough for those who are open to receiving.
- It is my right to share in this abundant Universe.
- I am ready to receive the abundance that is available through the Universe.
- It is my birthright to have an abundant and prosperous life.

- The prosperity that I have rights to is limitless.
- Abundance of all that is good is being drawn to me right now.
- The evidence of my prosperity and abundant life is being delivered to me today.
- Everything I do, draws affluence and abundance into my life
- I have unlimited resources working day and night to deliver the prosperity and abundance that is my birthright.
- I live in an abundant Universe.
- I choose abundance of all that is good in my life, and do so by releasing any and all barriers.
- I accept all abundance and prosperity with gratitude.
- I look forward to each day enthusiastically as an opportunity to create more abundance and prosperity.
- I am destined to have an abundance of love, wealth and prosperity in my life.
- Doing what I love, with love, is what creates abundance in my life.
- I live in unlimited lavish abundance. More and more flows to me with ease and certainty.
- I am worthy and deserving of prosperity, abundance and love.
- I allow and receive wealth, abundance and love into my life in all areas easily and effortlessly.

- I attract enough passive income to have the benefit of a prosperous, loving and luxurious lifestyle.

MY THOUGHTS:

Anytime Thoughts

- I'm so happy and grateful for all of the blessings life has brought me.
- I am going to have an AWESOME day. Fun, humor, peace and harmony all contribute to my day and my total health and wealth.
- I am a master at focusing my thoughts on what I desire, versus what I lack.
- My happy thoughts create happiness.
- My abundant thoughts create my abundance.
- My prosperous thoughts create prosperity.
- My positive thoughts create positive experiences.
- Empowering thoughts empower me.
- My thoughts that praise my health contribute to my good health.
- Destructive thoughts create destruction, which I am thankful to avoid.
- Through my unity with God, He totally supports my thoughts and what I choose to believe, and then delivers to me evidence of my belief.
- My thoughts become my beliefs and my beliefs become my reality, which is why all of my thoughts are empowering.
- I focus my thoughts on my desires, and I always get what I focus upon.
- I use my intuition to make wise choices.
- I choose everything in my life through my thoughts, which create my expectations that ultimately become my reality.

- My thoughts control my destiny. I control my thoughts. Therefore, I control my destiny.
- I envision all that I desire in life and create my outer world from within.
- I deserve all that I have because I give generously and add value to other people's lives.
- The fulfillment of my highest desires is unfolding constantly.
- I believe in miracles, therefore, I expect and receive miracles constantly.

Feelings and Love

- I love life. I look forward to every second of every day.
- Everything I do brings me happiness and joy.
- My life is getting better and better with each passing day.
- Happiness is abundant in my life.
- It feels great to smile and show appreciation and love to others.
- Smiling makes me and everyone I encounter happier.
- I feel better when I smile, and that's why I smile all the time.
- I decide each day how I'm going to feel, and I have decided to feel good everyday, for the rest of my life.
- I am united with God, and therefore, have His Infinite ability to create good in my life.
- I am meant for greatness. I am special and my unique individualism brings only what I can bring to this Universe.
- Life is like a joyous party, where everyone and everything is having a blast.
- The more I love myself, the more others love me, and the more happiness I feel within.
- I respect and love everyone, as I know that the more I love others, the more I will be loved.
- Love is the Universal Law that drives everything. I continue to find reasons to be more loving every day.

Creativity

- It is the synergy of differences among us that cause great things and experiences to happen.
- Today is going to be a fun day.
- I enjoy expressing myself creatively.
- I have new creative ideas every day.
- I am open to inspired thought and will act upon these creative thoughts as they arise.
- I have unlimited creative power, and am open to allow it to be expressed.
- My "gut" or inner voice has much wisdom.
- I am open and comfortable expressing my creativity.
- New creative ideas come to me frequently and easily.
- I am regularly presented with a new opportunity that sometimes is disguised as a challenge.
- There is only one moment to focus upon; the rest creatively unfolds as the Infinite Power that unites us all sets the forces in motion my intentions.
- My dreams and my visions of the future are joyous and are the building blocks for my future reality.
- I can create miracles with everyone and everything in the Universe benefiting, thanks to the Holy Spirit within me.

Gratitude

- I start and end my day thankful for my blessings.
- Life has been generous to me.
- I am truly blessed.
- I am thankful for every day of my life.
- Life has been awesome to me.
- I show others the love and gratitude they deserve.
- I am fortunate to have accomplished so much.
- Life is good.
- I am glad to be alive.
- I am grateful to others for the love they show me.
- I am overflowing with gratitude and praise for others.
- I am so fortunate and thankful for having an awesome family that was meant for greatness.
- I give thanks and praise frequently and easily.
- Thank you for my health.
- Thank you for my family and friends.
- Thank you for all of the blessings that I have.
- I am extremely fortunate to be where I am at in life.
- Gratitude for all that there is will set the forces in motion to experience more to be grateful for.

- I am grateful for all that I have and for all that I am yet to receive.

Growth

- There is no such thing as failure; it's just the feedback I need to ensure that I'm on the right course.
- When a situation doesn't go the way I expect, it's because God had something better in mind for me. The Infinite always knows best, and I trust that I will find the opportunity that was meant for me
- I am an exceptional manifestor…Success is guaranteed!
- Thank you for my freedom.
- I am meant for greatness.
- I can be who I will myself to be.
- I can achieve results through shear will.
- I can accomplish whatever I determine.
- I can will anything into my reality.
- Today is going to be unique, and I will enjoy the new, fresh experience of today.
- Today I will experience something I have never experienced before and I will be creatively expanding my knowledge and my life experiences, which will benefit me in time.
- Golden opportunities await me.
- Every experience I have benefits me. I am exceptional at finding each benefit and expanding upon them.

- I only experience good things in life.
- Change is always happening and it is change that creates my growth and opportunity.
- I open my mind to the possibilities that exist. Nothing is beyond my comprehension.
- Change is pleasant and exciting.
- I enjoy growing through new experiences.
- Everything that first appears doubtful becomes magnificent for me.

MY THOUGHTS:

CHAPTER 14

Personal Stories of Success

Both Bruce and Tammy are involved in groups that study *Universal Laws*. The following are stories that have been shared by some of the people in these groups and others that have made their acquaintance. Each story will share an experience with the **Law of Attraction** and other **Universal Laws**.

Interest in **Universal Laws** continues to grow at a phenomenal rate and group members share their stories, positive and motivational ideas, and other personal experiences and knowledge. (See credits for URL to these groups)

Here are a few of their stories:

<u>A Little Help Getting There</u>

"I was 28 years old and moving back to Florida with my wife and new born son at my side. My wife and I were both Florida natives and have our parents living there as well. I had just lost my grandmother and it made me realize that I didn't want my kids to grow up not knowing their grandparents. So off we went. I left a great position with a Fortune 500 company and I was scared, and at that time very self-defeating. I had three years of College but didn't finish and therefore

did not have a degree. I didn't believe in myself much and didn't think I had much to offer any company professionally, even though I had great success in the past. Looking back, it made no sense to have such self-doubt.

Within weeks of our transition, my mother in law advised me of an entry-level job opening in an industry I knew nothing about. I interviewed with the Vice President of General Operations and she reluctantly gave me the job. She legitimately was concerned about my lack of experience in the industry but she believed in me and as a result, I began to believe in myself.

Not long after I started with the company, I began to see that I could really have a positive impact in the industry and I actually believed it. Without even knowing about the Law of Attraction, I began to live it with my daily thoughts and prayers. I began to visualize myself making decisions as the next Vice President. I began to visualize the financial stability that having such a position would create. I pictured myself in new cars, with a new house, going on vacations that most people could only dream about. Then it started to happen, almost so quickly that it became surreal. One promotion after the next and wouldn't you know it, within 4.5 years of starting my Law of Attraction journey, I am a Vice President for the Sarasota Division of a Fortune 500 company. Needless to say, the Law of Attraction through my daily thoughts and prayers with God truly has worked *for me. It's POWERFUL STUFF!*

By the way, the Vice President of General Operations that believed in me just over four years ago was Tammy Lynch. We still work together today."

Rob Shiver, Brandon, Florida

Simple Things

"I can remember the first time I really thought about something I wanted and it showed up fairly quickly. I had just moved into a house and had very little furniture. The entry way was quite wide and I decided I needed a china hutch in there. So I wrote it down on a list I kept of things I wanted, knowing full well I would get it, just not knowing how and not even worrying about how. Within 2 weeks a friend calls me up and asks me if I wanted to use some of his furniture at my house, I'd be storing it for him while using it, including the china hutch. It fits perfectly in the entry way and looks great!

My car was wearing out so I put it out to the Universe that I wanted a new car by the end of the year. I did not know what kind of van I wanted, but I wanted it nice looking, running very well. Each time I got into my old car, I patted it on the dash board and thanked it for giving me such faithful service, then said "But now I am ready for a new vehicle and I am thankful that it is coming soon." I also envisioned me driving a van and being able to see above the tops of the other cars around me.

Within a short time, my car was really ready to quit working and I started saying, "I am thankful for my new van. It's really nice looking and runs really well." I kept saying that over and over.

Eight days later we have the nicest van! Very good looking and it runs perfectly!

That's it! I actually have had tons of experience getting what I wanted. I just never knew it was the "<u>Law of Attraction</u>" at work.

One time I really needed $575. I had no outside job. I worked at home, tending to family. I would sit quietly every day in a chair; eyes closed, with my hands on my lap, palms up. I would imagine money falling into my hands, adding up to $575. I had that money within one month. Someone gave it to me; someone I never expected would ever give me money. What fun! It works!"

Jean Lauzon

Positive Mental Attitude

"A friend said to me today," Dan I don't think I've ever heard you say one thing negative, are you inhuman?" My reply was this, "I have disappointments, failures and mistakes in my life, I only chose not to dwell on them, if something negative *pops in my head I instantly take a second close my eyes and think of something good while forcing a smile for one minute. This brief exercise instantly changes my mood if not just for the fact that I realize I am alone in a room with a big smile on my face for no reason!*

You see, I have found that positive and negative thoughts cannot exist in my mind at the same time and I have the power of which thought I entertain in my head. I have no control on outside forces and the images and thoughts, which enter my mind, but I can choose which ones to hold on to. Focusing on the moment enjoying the good around me and in my life right this second I bring myself to a happy place in which negativity is not welcome.

This for some people is very difficult. It is very hard to embrace the beauty around you if you are still entertaining thoughts of fear, remorse, guilt, and pride. If we are to be successful at bringing happiness into our present lives we must first let go of the negative emotions being fed from our past. We cannot begin to create a new happier self if we still hold on to the baggage of the former unhappy self. Self-discovery is a necessary process to forming contentment with ones self. We must first examine why we were the way we were if we are to discover who we want to be. After this thorough process we then are able to let go and begin anew. Without the negative emotions of who we were, we are now able to create who we want to become! The slate has been wiped clean; we are an empty canvass in which to paint the picture of our choosing. From this point if we chose to entertain negative thought we are again creating baggage blocking us from the reality of love. If we, from this point, chose only to focus on the positive we are inviting love into ourselves on every level. Try some self-discovery you might find that who you are is not who you want to be!!"

Dan Hoffman, Sarasota Florida

The Team!!

"I recently started as a Vice President for a new company. When I started my new position I went around and interviewed all my employees to see how the work environment and culture was before I arrived. I found that except for the new President that they had been regularly told how bad the situation was getting and that they could not see a how the company was going to make it. You could feel the drained energy and loss of focus. That was all going to change. On my first morning in my new position I spent the first couple of hours talking with Tammy Lynch (the President). I had just begun embracing some authors on positive thinking and living the "Laws of Attraction." Or so I thought. After my time with Tammy I was convinced of the success that we were about to achieve. **I truly believed** *that we were going to turn the team around and make great things happen. I started by seeking a new and positive message. It started simply when I introduced myself in my first staff meeting and told them "I believe*

that we are going to be the best, because I have met each one of you, and believe in you." I introduced my vision board to my staff and explained that we have to know what we are going to get. Believe that it is coming. Act as if it was already done. That next Sunday my preacher read this quote.

Mark 11:24 (GNB) "When you pray and ask for something, believe that you have received it, and you will be given whatever you ask for."

Now only two months into the New Year, our team has already reached 70% of the total production from the previous year. **We believe and we are achieving.** *"*

Jason Janssen, Bradenton Florida

Attracting Wealth

"A few months ago, my husband and I were struggling to only "GET BY" from paycheck to paycheck. It was so difficult. My mother was still ill and recovering from open-heart surgery... THEN I WAS INTRODUCED TO THE LAW OF ATTRACTION!!!!!!!!

We placed my order with the universe and BELIEVED it would manifest...My husband and I BOTH envisioned what we each desired and spoke of it like it were actually HERE, in the present. Our two teenage children thought we were a little nutty at first but now they are TRUE BELIEVERS IN THE LAW OF ATTRACTION.

I did a lot of writing in the beginning because I was such a negative thinker. It helped me to break old patterns of negativity. My husband on the other hand, has always been a positive person. He just focused on what would make him HAPPY. We both did visualizations every night before bed and kept a positive attitude during the day. It didn't manifest over night, but it did manifest.

My husband applied for a new job as a purchasing clerk at another company. The position was posted as $40,000 per year, which was not a dream job but it was a larger salary than his current job.

Then something very strange happened. The vice president of the company ran across his resume. He called my husband that evening at his work and asked him would he like to meet with him that evening. THIS IS A MULTIMILLION DOLLAR CORPORATION!!!!!!!!!! TERRY (MY HUSBAND) WAS FLOORED!!!!!!! He met with the VP of World Wide Inc. at his CONDO!!!

While he was there, my husband was offered an UNBELIEVABLE POSITION........ Executive Purchasing Director over 33 stores!!!!!!!!!! He has his own staff of 33 people!!!!!! This wasn't a position available within the company.......... THIS POSITION WASN'T EVEN AVAILABLE!!! IT'S A BRAND

NEW POSITION.... IT DIDNT EXIST... They weren't looking for anyone! IT JUST HAPPENED! HOW DO U EXPLAIN THAT OTHER THAN THE LAW OF ATTRACTION?!!!!!!!!!

My husband now has a 6 figure income including bonuses....... :O

Tammy..... we were scraping by....... I was literally searching for change to give to my children for lunch and snack money for school....I was in jeopardy of loosing my home because we were 2 months behind on the mortgage.... :'(I thank GOD for all I have been given!!!! I am truly blessed!!!!!

NOW MY TURN!!!!!!

I wanted to go back to work in my salon that I had to close because of my mothers illness. I'm a hairstylist and I have a true PASSION for what I do. I'm VERY creative, and artistic. I just thrive in that environment. BUT I DIDNT HAVE THE MONEYYYYYYYYYYY to reopen my salon.... then... I get a call.... from my Mother...

She asked me to come into town and look at this building for a salon. I was discouraged because I knew I didn't have the funds to open the salon but I thought what the heck, I'll go look at it anyway (this was before my husband had his new job).

I go look at the building and it's a small building but

PERFECT. I could only imagine all the great things I could do with the salon. My mother asked me if I liked it because there was another stylist that had been looking at the building. I said, Yeah, Mom I do like it but I just don't have the money right now.... SHE SAID TO ME, "That's ok, I've already leased the building!!!!!!!!!!!!!!!!!!!!!" It's in your name. Pay me when you can. I SAT DOWN THEN AND THERE AND CRIED and hugged my Mother.

WELL SINCE THEN. I've repaid my Mom, we're putting together my new salon and Terry is working and he is SOOOOOOOOO HAPPY NOW!!!!!! He glows when he comes home from work... Not only because of the money, but because he is feeling CHALLENGED.

If anyone ever says that there is no such thing as the Law of Attraction I really feel sorry for him or her. I have lived it. I am living proof. Tammy, thank you so much for everything!!!!!! THANK YOU THANK YOU THANK YOU! I am sooooooooo grateful to have you in my life!

I'm sorry if this was LONG but I just had to share my joy with you and to thank you for helping me along the path of LOA!!!!!!!

PEACE, LOVE AND LIGHT TO YOU MY FRIEND!!!!!"

Darla

My Dream Home

"I looked at a townhome about six months ago and was fearful to offer the price for it. I live in Lafayette and due to the hurricane that we recently had in the area home prices were crazy high. So I underbid and lost the home. Every time I looked at another home I was reminded about the one that got away. So I began focusing upon finding the perfect place, like the one that got away and continued to patiently continue looking for the perfect place.

Well, I was invited to a Christmas party on the same street as the perfect place that I lost, and IT WAS FOR SALE. This time I got it. I signed the papers the next day and had no hesitation whatsoever. It was there in escrow for me, just waiting.

I am moving to my perfect place in a couple of weeks! The difference now is that I have seen all of the contrasting places that I didn't want and my desire became focused on what I did want. I am completely comfortable with offering what I offered and knowing that it is the perfect place for me."

Robert Ellender, Lafayette, Louisiana

I Live Like It's Already Here

"Every Sunday, I decide on one thing I want to receive that week. I have done this for 6 weeks now & everything I wanted showed up. From seeing a friend I hadn't seen in over a year, to an extra $100.00, it all shows up.

I live like it's already here & appreciate every moment."

Amy

The Money Showed Up

"I always look at a situation with joy as I see it unfold and then trace the synchronicities that enable my desired manifestation. I will only give a couple of examples, and I must say that I am having so much fun with the Law of Attraction.

First of all, my invitation to this group on MySpace, as I desire to attract more like-minded people into my life.

Second, and this was such fun. I needed a new glass storm door for my front door. For 2 weeks, every time I walked through that door, I visualized opening, walking through and then closing the brand new door. I went shopping to price the door and within 2 weeks a check came in the mail for the amount I needed for the door.

Such fun :)"

Sheila

Adopt A Cat

"I just learned about the LOA this month but LAST MONTH my fiancé and I decided we were going to

adopt a cat from the humane society. We started pondering what type of cat we wanted.... a larger size cat, already de-clawed, loving, lazy, won't jump on the counters, no interest in eating plants or scratching up the furniture. We both kept on thinking of this cat that we would love to have. Then one day we decided to go to Agway- a plant store. Usually they have a cage there from the Humane Society with an animal in there for adoption...they are affiliated. Well, I don't remember why we had to go there...probably for something that could have waited to get. I went over to see what animal was in there this time and there he was...a 20 lb cat, already de-clawed, neutered, lazy, extremely loving, no interest in jumping on counters and knocking things off, eating plants and LOVES people and LOVES to be pet. HE WAS PERFECT.... he was everything we dreamed of in a cat. We put in an application and got him 2 days later.

It wasn't until after I learned about the LOA that I realized it that we manifested him.

It is so interesting to think.... my fiancé and I didn't know we wanted a cat until a week before we got our kitty that we have now for about a month and a half...yet he is 3 years old.... It was like he was meant to be adopted by us (no one else wanted him) but he was born years earlier than when we realized what we wanted.

The universe is truly very mysterious!"

BrideZilla

South Barre, Vermont

Meaningful Pictures

"A very recent example I have is from last week. On Christmas morning, I sent my 16-year-old daughter off to spend the day with her mom. I then spent some time alone after she had left thinking of how fast the time has gone by and wishing I had more pictures of her when she was very young. I have raised her on my own since she was 6, and had no pictures of us together prior to that.

I thought about it throughout the day. When my daughter returned later that evening, she had a box full of pictures that her mother had given to her to give to me. Pictures I never knew existed from before her mom and I had separated. It was the first time in 10 years that I had received anything like that from her mother. What a "coincidence" to get them on the day I had put such thought and emotion into the idea...

Everything in our life, good or bad, is through the law of attraction. Some things just have more meaning, more value and stand out more than others. I have intentionally attracted some great things into my life, but often it is the simple, little things that mean the most."

No Name, LAKE STEVENS, WASHINGTON

Going to Test Drive A New Car

"As I learn about LOA I see it everywhere. It's jumping off the pages of books that seemingly have nothing to do with it. People are talking about it everywhere I go. Positive people are showing up in my life and I'm learning from them every day.

I've changed my attitude and my entire experience. Today I'm going to go test drive the new car I want. This is fun! Life is good!"

Kelby

Listen in Unwanted Intentions

"I like to write my intentions - because it helps to focus me. Recently I wrote an intention to clear my clutter. I also wrote an intention to do some remodeling and have the money I need to do so.

While shopping for Christmas gifts, I came across a book that really got my energy going in the direction of the clutter clearing. We've had lots of snow; being inside more gave me additional motivation. I took some extra time off around the New Year holiday and made serious in-roads into unloading what no longer is useful to me.

Because of the snow, the aluminum awning that covered the entrance to my home collapsed - so I get to remodel my front entrance, with some help from my homeowner's insurance!

An important point is that I have been "wishing" that front entrance were different for a long time, but had a lot of inertia around changing it... It has been a profound lesson in the effects of "unconscious" intentions!"

Trish

The Universe Rearranges Itself

"I started reading Think And Grow Rich by Napoleon Hill about a month ago and I've been studying its pages continually ever since. I wanted to know the "Secret" that he talks about in the introduction, more than anything else in the world. I wanted to know it! I wanted to use it in my life! Because from the experiences that were in that book I KNEW it had to power to change people's lives more than anything else I had ever heard of.

As I was reading I had the inspiration to sit down and write out a definite goal of the amount of money I intend to have by August 31 of this year. Why that date? I'm leaving on an LDS mission after that for two years. So I have a definite deadline to accomplish my goals. My intention is to earn $200, 000 by August 31. I'm only 18 but that doesn't matter. I'm starting a financial services franchise and my broker dealer has set promotion guidelines, etc. to be able to set up a business. I sat down and wrote out a business plan that was going to get me that $200, 000 in eight months. Involved in that was the requirement I put on myself to be promoted twice before the end of February.

Nobody does that. The fastest promotion I've ever heard of has happened in about three months.

Well, here's where the Law of Attraction came in. I didn't know how I was going to do it; I just KNEW I was going to. I knew it! That's all I cared about. I was going to do it, no matter what.

About a week after I wrote down my definite chief aim of having made $200, 000 in the next eight months, one of my colleagues gave me a copy of "The Secret". I watched it with my parents and it totally turned my life around. Ideas I was starting to grasp by reading Think And Grow Rich suddenly became crystal clear and full of meaning. I decided to put it to the test.

The next day I had an important meeting up at the office. I don't own a car at the moment so I had no way of getting there but I told my colleagues I would show up on time. I went through the process of visualization and focusing on being at the meeting. And guess what?

I didn't get a ride to that meeting. I got a ride to a meeting that was an hour and a half later. I walked into the office and began apologizing for not being at the meeting when one of the guys stopped me and said "Hey don't worry about it. The meeting's been rescheduled."

I visualized being at that meeting. I will still be at that meeting. It's amazing to me how that happened! But

163

here's the even bigger example, the one that has a lot more meaning to me:

So I was at that later meeting right.. The meeting ended and we were about ready to go home when one of the leaders up at the firm stepped up and announced that "oh by the way, as an incentive the promotion guidelines for the next two months, (through the end of February) have been reduced by about 90%."

When I made the goal to be promoted twice I didn't know how it was going to happen. By all practical purposes I'd have to be one of the very top personal producers worldwide for that to happen at the usual standards. But then the Universe just started rearranging itself to fit my needs, to cater to my wants and desires.

To make my dreams come true. And THAT is why I know the Law of Attraction is true. I could go through countless other examples that have happened in the past couple weeks but I think I've said enough. :) Just look all around you, the LOA is present everywhere, in everyone, everything. It's so powerful I can't hope to ever be able to comprehend it on this mortal plane."

Bryan

Do Coincidences Exist?

"I was introduced to the Law of Attraction by the film The Secret which I saw for the first time in October last year, I think it was. I would like to share the story of what happened the day after I watched The Secret for the first time.

During the film, when I heard them talk about thinking of what you want, instead of what you don't want and especially after the chapter on visualization I thought of a certain car I've been dreaming of for 7 years already. The first time I saw this car, I knew one day I'll have such a car. It's a Jeep Cherokee 4x4 in dark blue.

My dream was to get the chance to sit in that car, so that I know what it's like. Really, I only wanted to sit in it. Meanwhile the new versions of that car look weird, I don't like them. But there is another car, a Land Rover, which looks pretty much like the old Jeeps, and they exist in that beautiful dark blue color as well. If I had to choose between an old Jeep and a new Land Rover I'd take the Land Rover. So during the film I was thinking of that car and visualized what it would be like to sit in that car.

The day after that I accompanied my father to visit clients. He works as an estate agent and sometime I help him out. The couple we visited had a house and a piece of land for sale. After we finished the house the young man took us to the piece of land in his own car.

Guess what car that was!!!!!!!! A dark blue Land Rover, exactly the one I was thinking about.

Seven years I dreamt of sitting in that car and suddenly, out of the blue, boom! It happened! The day after I visualized that car so intensively while watching The Secret.

Also funny to mention is the fact this young man (about the same age as me) almost looked like me! We wore exactly the same cloths! Jeans, a dark blue pullover and a black vest. We even had the same type of shoes! So while I was sitting in the back watching this young man drive 'my car' it was easy for me to imagine that it's me behind the steering wheel. Well, his hair was a lot shorter then mine, but hey! :-)

There is more to tell, and more important stuff than the dream of sitting in a particular type of car, but this event really made me think.

What was that? Was it a mere coincidence or was it the LOA? Do coincidences even exist?"

Nicole

THIS JOB!

"Less than year ago my partner and I (we own a media company in Toronto Ontario Canada) saw the secret, about June I would say.

We decided that we wanted to attract a job like that.

We wanted to be able to lend our creativity to a project that we truly loved, and that used all of our talents effectively. We definitely did not have the connections at the time, and we did not know of any similar projects in production.

Now, we are working on this MAGNIFICENT film, PassItOn that features John Assaraf from the Secret and many other notable teachers, speakers and motivators.

It is more than a dream come true."

Jennifer

Paintings Selling

"I had not sold a painting in over a year. I became aware of the Law of Attraction and gratitude. So on a trip to Denver, Colorado, I began saying "I am so happy and grateful that my paintings are sold."

When my wife and I returned to Utah from our trip to Denver, there was a message on my phone from a gallery telling me to come and pick up a check. My paintings had been in this gallery for over two and a half years. This was the first time this gallery had sold one of my paintings. Over the course of that month, I sold 8 more paintings.

As I am painting now, I keep saying to myself the

affirmation that my paintings are sold. I have a friend that I take my paintings to and in most every case now, he gives me a call within a few days telling me to come and pick up a check."

Doyle Shaw

CONCLUSION

What It All Comes Down To!

You are the *"Master"* of your destiny. Since you control your thoughts, you control your destiny. Thought is the seed of reality! By focusing only on those things you want rather then the things you don't want, you guarantee that the reality you are experiencing is in line with the reality you desire.

> *"Faith is the substance of things hoped for, the evidence of things not seen."*

Faith is an actual substance, it is an energy, it is the form that the plasmatic substance of the Universe is magnetized to which is eventually manifest as your desire or goal.

Initially, you start with a thought and you sew that thought which will eventually become a feeling inside of you, *"the evidence of things not seen."* As you continue to nurture the thought and expand the feeling inside, you will find that the manifestation of that which you desire will be imminent.

Faith is, believing in something so strongly you bring it to reality. The "I" within you has the power to achieve anything you can dream of. Believe in the

"I" within you and everything you desire - Health, Wealth, Love and *"harmonic abundance"* will be yours.

The title of this book is "Mastery of Abundant Living." The purpose of this book is to help you *"Master the Key to the Law of Attraction"*.

Mastery - *great skillfulness and knowledge of some subject or activity*

The **Law of Attraction** knows no religion, no race, no ethnic origin or any other type of discrimination. This *law* is simply that, a law that you can apply to whatever you believe! It is the same *law* for everyone anywhere in the world and actually the whole Universe. It doesn't matter your gender, race, religion or sex, it is the same *law* of everyone.

The only difference in how the **Law of Attraction** works towards ones benefit is the application of it by the individual. All you have to do is apply the principles of the **Law of Attraction** and you *"Will"* change you life.

Everything around you is energy. Even your body is *"energy."* The very second you have a thought; energy is reacting to that thought even across the Universe. It is not hard to understand then that when you apply thought to your body that the very energy that makes up your body immediately reacts to your thoughts.

To transform your body, your life, your family, your love life, your health, your wealth or anything else in and around you, your first step is to change your thoughts. Since thoughts transcend time and space, immediately when you have a thought, your Universe and everything around you starts to rearrange itself.

If you don't want your future to be the same as your present, then change your thoughts from those of the past. This is the time for you to create new thoughts that are self-empowering and not self-defeating.

Simply believe in the "I" within you and your unity with the *Infinite* which has unlimited resources. Who you are, is a reflection of your thoughts and beliefs. It's your character, your environment, and even your appearance. When you begin to come to the understanding of this tremendous realization that you are in fact part of the *Eternal Energy*, and the "I" within you is truly united with the *Infinite*, that you are one with the *Creator* and the same in quality and kind, then you will understand the transcendental possibilities and that your life is at your command!

MY THOUGHTS:

CREDITS & RESOURCES

Law of Attraction groups Moderated by Bruce Goldwell and Tammy Lynch on MySpace.

"Master Key"
Moderated by Tammy Lynch
Groups.myspace.com/masterkey

"Mastery of Abundant Living"
Moderated by Bruce Goldwell
Groups.myspace.com/masteryofabundantliving

Other resources:

Law of Attraction Conferences
www.LawofAttractionConferences.com

"Mastery of Abundant Living" Web Site
www.MasterySource.com
Inspirational videos, posters, calendars, and much more!

Added thanks to:

James Wallace
Quantum Physics
"Meta-wealth, The Art of Conscious Wealth"
www.myspace.com/metawealth

Tammy Lynch

Tammy Lynch is a national speaker and instructor and has been developing training materials and courses since the late 1990's.

Although Tammy is a novice author, she brings a unique perspective to the application of Universal Laws as it has been a study of hers since the 80's. Tammy contributes her success to her own personal drive and desire, the support she receives from her son, and her application of Universal Laws. She was raised in St. Clair Shores, Michigan and is currently residing in Florida.

Bruce Goldwell

Bruce Goldwell is the author of "*The Door To Super Achievement*", "*The Power of Choice*" and a book series for young readers titled "*Dragon Keepers*" as well as a songwriter, teacher, motivator, entrepreneur, inventor and producer. The father of six children with four grandchildren, he was raised in West Palm Beach, Florida and is currently residing in Utah.

Printed in the United States
86941LV00002B/7/A